Tom Kerridge

Cooks BRITAIN

To Bef and Acey xx

And to all the British farmers and producers

Tom Kerridge

Cooks BRITAIN

A JOURNEY THROUGH THE BEST OF BRITISH FOOD

BLOOMSBURY ABSOLUTE

LONDON · OXFORD · NEW YORK · NEW DELHI · SYDNEY

Our Great British Food Nation 6

Vegetables 16

Fish & Shellfish 74

Meat & Poultry 116

Dairy 172

Fruit 224

Index 264

Our Great British Food Nation

We all have treasured memories involving food. Probably my first understanding of how we connect with food and farming was pick-your-own fruit – strawberries, raspberries and gooseberries. As a kid, it was the perfect introduction to how food and the seasons work together.

A strawberry that has ripened very slowly over the summer in Scotland, where daylight hours are longer compared to further south, has a much more intense flavour and unbelievable sweetness. Freshly picked, it's one of the most incredible taste experiences I've had, and is more exciting to me than most of the exotic fruits you get all year round in the supermarket.

> Wherever you are in Britain, you'll find amazing people producing incredible ingredients. With beautiful fruits and veg – and some of the best meat and dairy in the world – these recipes showcase their unbeatable qualities.

From sweet, freshly picked peas, which I've paired with creamy burrata, an intense mint and basil oil, crispy Parma ham and crunchy sourdough toasts (see page 36); to beautifully rich, oily mackerel with crunchy pickled cucumber (on page 100); and succulent lamb rump with rocket salsa verde (see page 149), it's time to celebrate how great British produce really is.

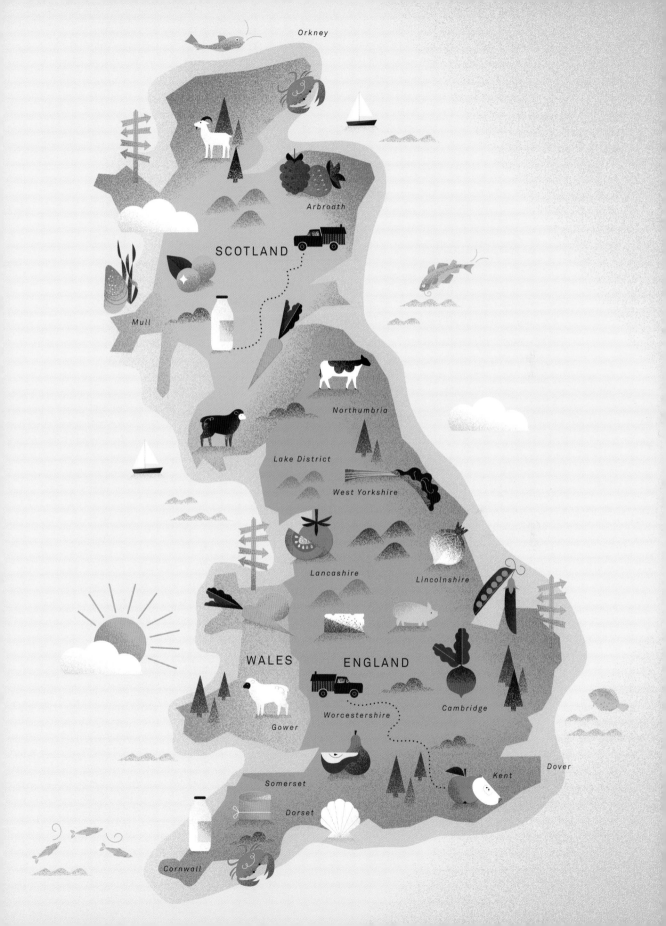

Orkney

Arbroath

SCOTLAND

Mull

Northumbria

Lake District

West Yorkshire

Lancashire

Lincolnshire

WALES   ENGLAND

Worcestershire

Cambridge

Gower

Kent

Dover

Somerset

Dorset

Cornwall

One of the reasons we have such a fantastic range of home-grown ingredients in Britain is because we're lucky enough to live in a climate defined by four strong seasons. We might all like to complain about the wet weather, long winters and the brief few weeks of intense heat we call summer, but it's these contrasting weather patterns that drive the diversity of what we are able to grow and farm throughout the year. It also means we're only ever a few weeks away from a whole new range of fantastic ingredients to explore in our cooking!

Although modern farming methods mean most of what we buy is available all year round, buying fresh and in season is almost always going to guarantee better-quality, tastier produce.

Those first bright green spears of asparagus that appear in very early spring are prized for their fantastic flavour. Sweet squashes, salad veg and fragrant berries through the summer give way to crisp apples and pears that have taken months to ripen in the sun in the autumn, which is also the season for wild mushrooms. With the first frosts, we turn to those dense, irony, rich brassicas and root vegetables that keep us going through the winter months.

There's always something to look forward to. And, just when we're starting to get fed up with the cold weather and are craving something lighter in our meals, the sun starts to shine and we're able to enjoy those fresh tastes of spring again. It's the perfect balance of plenty of rain, and just enough sunshine. We often forget that meat, fish and seafood have a seasonality too. There's a reason we have Easter lamb and crab sandwiches on our summer holidays.

It's not only the changing British seasons that provide ideal conditions for so much great produce. The landscape of Britain also works to our benefit in a similar way. All those undulating fields of lush green grass you see throughout the South and Southwest are perfect for cows to roam and graze, producing incredible beef and dairy. In East Anglia, where the land is flatter and the soil sandier, we grow lots of delicious veg including some of the best potatoes and carrots you'll ever taste, and it's also perfectly suited to raising pigs.

Together, the terrain and climate in Britain work in an endlessly cyclical, uniquely special way, providing us with an ever-changing abundance of food to cook, eat and enjoy.

Further north and across Wales, sheep climb over hills, getting strong and muscular. And, being an island nation surrounded by coast, we are never far away from a huge variety of freshly caught fish and seafood. The deep, cold North Atlantic waters off Scotland are home to cod and haddock, while shallower shores are where you can find crabs, mussels, oysters and clams.

Let's celebrate our heroes

When I'm putting together a new recipe, I first decide what's going to be the hero of the dish, the central ingredient around which the rest of the meal is built. Maybe it's a juicy steak (see page 137), some beautiful fresh broad beans (see page 30) or some sharp and salty blue cheese (see page 188). I then look to balance the flavours and profiles – to enhance, support and bring out all the unique qualities of that main ingredient. And that's how the chapters in this book are organised too.

Each chapter focuses on celebrating the very best of British fruit and veg, meat, dairy, fish and seafood, with recipes based around a single amazing British ingredient.

It's also how I think a lot of us cook at home on a daily basis: we open the fridge and see a packet of mince or a box of blueberries and wonder what we can do with them!

The chapter titles also mirror the key areas of farming that have made up the backbone of British industry for hundreds of years. British identity has been entwined with farming and agriculture for generations, and we can be proud of having some of the best farmers in the world.

As more of us move towards urban living, we can find ourselves becoming increasingly distanced from the impact of the seasons on our day to day, and the vital role these industries have played in the livelihoods of so many people. But for those of us living outside of cities, life can still feel very much dictated to by the natural world and the rhythms of the farming year.

A rapidly growing food culture here in Britain has also influenced changes in the farming industry. It's not only in high-end restaurant kitchens that we have access to fantastic produce; over the past twenty or thirty years, the food scene in Britain has changed so much, and we've all started to demand a lot more from the food we eat. As a result, there have been some brilliant advances in sustainable farming practices, and it's almost like we've gone full circle in many areas, moving away from high-tech mass production towards an appreciation of more traditional artisan methodology.

From supermarkets to farm shops,
everyone is now able to enjoy better food,
and I love seeing how much more choice
we have when we do our weekly shop.

As our farmers and producers continue to face challenging times, with costs increasing across the board, it's more important than ever to try and support them whenever we can by buying British and, where possible, shopping locally.

Sometimes we forget that every product we buy, from a bag of frozen peas to some sausages or a pot of yoghurt, has been cared for by a real human, every step of the way, who has a family just like we do. It's personal.

We have an impressive farming heritage and the environment and skills to grow and care for a huge range of fruits, vegetables and livestock – let's champion our farmers and keep those traditions going strong for as long as we can.

Changing the food culture

Years ago, British cooking used to feel quite regional, but it's no longer about a geographical food divide, it's food for everyone wherever you are. Roast dinners are just as popular on Sunday lunch tables in the South as they are up North in the original home of the Yorkshire pudding.

Fish and chips is definitely still a favourite seaside treat, but even in the middle of Birmingham – the most landlocked place in Britain – you can get fresh fish every day. The same puddings show up on menus all over the country – a crumble is just as delicious wherever you are in Britain (try my Blackberry, pear and apple crumble on page 253).

As consumers, we are also now very comfortable about having international influences in our cooking and it's brilliant to see how up for trying new things we all are – we're no longer a meat and two veg nation!

These recipes aren't about highlighting specific dishes from around Britain; they're showcasing the very best of British ingredients wherever you live, using simple preparation methods and clean bold flavours to bring out their unique qualities.

Many of the recipes are very simple and pared back: Charred leeks with hazelnuts and vinaigrette (page 29) or Pickled radish and sea bass crudo (page 35). While in others, you'll see I have borrowed flavours and preparation techniques from abroad, where I think they will help enhance our British ingredients. There are American barbecue influences and Middle Eastern grilling skills in the Barbecued pork tomahawk steak (page 120) and Lamb shish with garlic and mint yoghurt (page 154), and Japanese flavours alongside the halibut on page 114.

Meanwhile, the fruit chapter is a pure celebration of British sweet dishes, like Plum and apple cobbler enhanced with vanilla and warm spices (on page 254) and Strawberry and elderflower trifle with its homemade fruit jelly (on page 240). Above all, these are all uncomplicated, robust and generous recipes, with our finest British ingredients at their centre.

Food connects us

Remove the complications of work and life, and what we are all needing is a bit more of the fundamentals of what make us smile – and a lot of that is a return to Mother Nature, with more of a connection to the food we eat. In unstable, unsettling times – which we are all living through right now – good food, cooked using honest, quality ingredients from close to where we live is an amazingly simple way of reconnecting us to what's important. It grounds us.

> British food is constantly moving, changing through the seasons, and we have so much incredible produce grown here, right on our doorsteps.

I encourage you to look around you, support your local farmers and producers and enjoy more of our great British ingredients.

Vegetables

Where eating seasonally really makes a big difference is to the quality and taste of our veg. Modern farming methods mean the seasons can be stretched a little, using techniques like growing in poly-tunnels, but even if it's possible to buy tomatoes in winter, they're never going to taste as good as those that ripen in the middle of summer.

And then there are certain veg that you simply can't get all year round, and these are the ones I look forward to the most: asparagus in the spring kicks off the first of the veg seasons, while Brussels sprouts, iron-rich kales and those big, hearty root veg come in at the end.

As a chef, it's what makes cooking with vegetables so exciting; there's always something new around the corner, it's a constantly changing set of ingredients to play with.

The sheer variety of veg that's native to Britain is incredible and each one brings something special to a meal. Whether it's colour or texture or flavour, or a combination of all three, veg is no longer seen as something that only sits on the side of your plate, an accompaniment but not the main event. Now, vegetables can be the central feature and I'm all for it. You have to think a little more creatively when it comes to putting a meal together that's based around veg, and how you prepare and cook vegetables varies as much as the ingredients themselves. You can get away with cooking summer veg very lightly – or even eating them raw: fresh peas straight from the vine, for example, or quickly blanched broad beans (page 30). Whereas those dense root veg need a bit more attention.

Root vegetables are pure science fiction to me: they grow in secret, underground, so you can't see what they're up to and the only way to know they're ready is to pull them up. Then you need to peel away that thick protective outer skin to reveal their bold flavours and incredible vibrant colours: vivid whites, yellows and oranges, deep reds and purples of celeriac, turnips, swede, carrots and beetroot. There's nothing else like them. As an ingredient, they need to be cooked for longer, but they're also more forgiving – so don't worry too much about overcooking them as they'll only get sweeter and more tender. Celeriac is fantastic in the soup on page 69, so do give it a go.

In Britain, we are seeing a return to some of the more traditional methods of farming vegetables, including multi-crop fields where more than one crop is grown in a field either at the same time or at different times of the year, and crop rotation, where what's grown changes each year. It's a much more sustainable way of growing veg, as it helps keep the soil nutrient-rich.

In turn this improves the quality of what we grow. It means the veg we eat is all that more nutritious and we're growing with the seasons too.

The recipes in this chapter take us all the way through the year, from light summer dishes to warming winter meals, all with the best of British veg at their core. If you aren't familiar with kohlrabi, give the remoulade on page 60 a go: it has the most incredible peppery taste and crunchy texture – perfect with rich smoked salmon and slices of dark rye bread.

Lightly char-grilling asparagus is a great technique to enhance its earthy bitterness, which works beautifully alongside its natural sweetness and the richness of the accompanying hollandaise (see page 23). Broccoli is on most people's shopping list throughout the year, and I've prepared it in two very different ways depending on the season: a simple summery traybake with feta (on page 50) and a heartier pasta dish (see page 52).

The creamy herb and potato bake (on page 70) is a bit like a classic dauphinoise but using ricotta for a lighter taste and texture. It's still a deep, thick cook though, perfect in the winter; just put it in the middle of the table and spoon it out. These recipes show that you can do incredible things with veg and they definitely deserve to be at the centre of more of our mealtimes.

Roast tomatoes with whipped feta and flatbreads

The quality of British tomatoes has improved over the years and we now enjoy a lot of varieties. Fresh-from-the-vine tomatoes will always get my vote as they boast the perfect balance of sweetness and acidity. Flatbreads, whipped feta and pesto complement intensely sweet roasted tomatoes superbly. This is summer on a plate!

Serves 4 as a lunch

Flatbreads
350g strong white bread flour, plus extra to dust
1½ tsp salt
3 sprigs of oregano, leaves picked and finely chopped
1 tsp caster sugar
1 tbsp extra virgin olive oil
7g sachet instant dried yeast (about 1½ tsp)

Roasted tomatoes
750g Rosso sweet cherry tomatoes
4 garlic cloves, thickly sliced
4 sprigs of oregano
80ml extra virgin olive oil
3 tbsp red wine vinegar
Salt and freshly ground pepper

Whipped feta
350g feta
200g Greek yoghurt
1 tbsp extra virgin olive oil

To finish
4 tbsp pesto
4 tsp aged balsamic vinegar
A handful of basil leaves

1 Preheat the oven to 200°C/180°C Fan/Gas 6.

2 To make the flatbread dough, sift the flour and salt into a large bowl and stir through the oregano. Pour 225ml warm water into a jug and add the sugar, yeast and extra virgin olive oil. Stir well and leave to stand for 5 minutes, then pour onto the dry ingredients and mix well to form a dough.

3 Transfer the dough to a lightly floured surface and knead for a few minutes until smooth and springy to the touch. Wipe out the bowl, place the dough back in it, cover and leave in a warm place for an hour or until doubled in size.

4 Tip the tomatoes onto a large oven tray. Scatter with the garlic and oregano, trickle on the extra virgin olive oil and season well. Roast on the middle oven shelf for 20 minutes.

5 Meanwhile, for the whipped feta, put the feta, yoghurt and extra virgin olive oil into a small food processor along with a good pinch each of salt and pepper and blitz until smooth. Cover and place in the fridge until needed.

6 When the tomatoes are roasted, remove them from the oven, trickle over the wine vinegar and stir gently. Set aside.

7 Knock back the risen dough and divide into 4 equal pieces. Shape into balls and leave to prove for 30 minutes. Roll each ball into a 20cm round. Heat a griddle pan up over a high heat. Cook the flatbreads in batches for 2–3 minutes on each side. Keep warm in the oven while you cook the rest.

8 Divide the whipped feta between 4 plates and top with the roasted tomatoes. Dot with the pesto and trickle over the tomato cooking juices and aged balsamic. Scatter over the basil leaves and serve, with the hot flatbreads. Alternatively, you can serve everything on top of the flatbreads.

Asparagus, poached eggs and hollandaise

British asparagus is unrivalled and deserves to be celebrated during its all-too-short season. It takes no time to cook, so your attention will mostly be turned to poaching the eggs to perfection and making my quick and easy hollandaise. A posh brunch, indeed!

Serves 2 as a lunch or brunch

4 large free-range eggs
1 tbsp cider vinegar
250g asparagus spears
  (about 10)
1 tbsp extra virgin olive oil
2 thick slices of sourdough
Salt and freshly ground
  pepper

Hollandaise
150ml butter
1 banana shallot, finely
  chopped
2 tbsp cider vinegar
2 tbsp white wine
3 black peppercorns
2 sprigs of tarragon, plus
  1 tbsp finely chopped
  leaves to finish
2 free-range egg yolks
2 tbsp double cream
Juice of ½ lemon, or to taste

1. To make the hollandaise, first clarify the butter. Melt the butter in a small saucepan and bring to the boil. Take off the heat and set aside for 2 minutes, then pour through a muslin-lined sieve into a bowl to remove the solids.

2. Put the shallot, cider vinegar, wine, peppercorns and tarragon sprigs into a small pan, bring to the boil and let bubble to reduce by half. Pass through a sieve into a heatproof bowl and whisk in the egg yolks, cream and 2 tbsp water.

3. Set the bowl over a pan of gently simmering water and whisk the mixture vigorously for a few minutes until it is pale and thickened. Add the clarified butter a little at a time, whisking after each addition. Season with salt and lemon juice to taste and take off the heat.

4. To cook the eggs, bring a pan of water to a gentle simmer and add the 1 tbsp cider vinegar. Crack the eggs into the water and poach gently for 3 minutes or until the whites are firm.

5. Meanwhile, heat a medium frying pan over a medium heat then add the asparagus with 2 tbsp water and the extra virgin olive oil. Season with salt and pepper and cook for 2–3 minutes until the asparagus is tender and the water has bubbled away.

6. While the eggs and asparagus are cooking, toast the sourdough slices on both sides and place on warm plates. As soon as the eggs are ready, carefully remove them from the pan with a slotted spoon and drain on kitchen paper.

7. Lay the asparagus on the warm toast and top each serving with a couple of poached eggs. Add the chopped tarragon to the hollandaise and give it a whisk. Spoon over the poached eggs and finish with a grinding of pepper to serve.

Asparagus, pecorino and lemon pasta

Embrace the start of spring with this easy pasta featuring luscious asparagus. This is one of those fabulously speedy dishes — by the time your pasta is cooked, the sauce is also ready. The chilli and lemon provide a zesty kick and the pecorino and basil add heaps of savoury flavour.

Serves 2 as a main

250g dried linguine
350g asparagus spears
2 tbsp extra virgin olive oil
1 garlic clove, finely chopped
A pinch of dried chilli flakes
Finely grated zest and juice
   of 1 lemon
50g pecorino, finely grated
30g cold butter, cut into cubes
A handful of basil leaves
   (optional)
Salt and freshly ground
   pepper

1   Bring a large saucepan of water to the boil for your pasta and season liberally with salt.

2   Cut two-thirds of the asparagus into 4–5cm pieces. Shave the remaining spears into long strips using a vegetable peeler; set these aside for later.

3   Tip the pasta into the boiling salted water, stir it gently and cook for about 8 minutes until *al dente* (tender but still firm to the bite).

4   In the meantime, place a medium frying pan over a medium heat and add the extra virgin olive oil. When it is hot, add the asparagus pieces, along with the garlic and chilli flakes, and sauté for 2 minutes. Scoop out the asparagus pieces and set aside on a plate.

5   Drain the linguine as soon as it is cooked, saving a ladleful of the cooking water. Add the linguine to the frying pan with the saved cooking water and lemon juice. Add half of the lemon zest and most of the grated pecorino. Toss the pan until the sauce emulsifies and coats the pasta.

6   Add the cooked asparagus back to the pan along with the strips of raw asparagus and toss the pan or stir to mix. Now add the butter and continue to stir until the sauce is silky. Season with salt and pepper to taste. Take the pan off the heat and toss through the basil leaves, if using.

7   Divide the pasta between warmed serving bowls and sprinkle with the remaining lemon zest and pecorino to serve.

Leek and potato soup with crispy potato topping

The mild sweetness of leeks can truly enhance the flavour of a dish and there are plenty of British leek growers keeping our shelves well stocked with this hardy veg. This silky-textured soup is comforting and satisfying, and the crispy potato topping makes it extra special.

Serves 4 as a lunch or starter

3 leeks, trimmed and washed
2 tbsp olive oil
50g butter
3 garlic cloves, sliced
500g Maris Piper potatoes,
    peeled and diced
4 sprigs of thyme, leaves
    picked
1 litre vegetable or
    chicken stock
150ml double cream, plus
    extra to drizzle
100ml whole milk
3 tbsp crème fraîche
2 tbsp finely chopped chives
Salt and freshly ground
    pepper

Crispy potato garnish
20g butter
1 tbsp extra virgin olive oil
150g Maris Piper potato,
    peeled and finely diced

1 Slice the leeks thinly into 5mm thick slices. Heat the olive oil and butter in a large saucepan over a medium-high heat. When the butter is melted and foaming, add the leeks and cook for 5 minutes or until softened. Add the garlic and cook for a further 3 minutes.

2 Add the potatoes, thyme and stock to the saucepan and bring to a simmer. Cook gently for 20 minutes or until the potatoes are softened.

3 Meanwhile, prepare the potato garnish. Heat the butter and extra virgin olive oil in a small frying pan over a medium-high heat. When the butter is melted and foaming, add the diced potato and stir well. Cook for 8 minutes or until the potato cubes are golden, cooked through and crispy.

4 To finish the soup, tip the contents of the saucepan into a jug blender and blitz until smooth. Pour the soup back into the saucepan and stir in the cream and milk. Season with salt and pepper to taste. Just before serving, stir through the crème fraîche.

5 Ladle the soup into warmed bowls and drizzle a little cream over each portion. Sprinkle with chopped chives and garnish with the crispy potatoes to serve.

Charred leeks with hazelnuts and vinaigrette

These charred leeks can be prepared indoors or on the barbecue. The key is to get them well blackened, which will result in a tender interior and an irresistible depth of flavour. I finish them with grated hard-boiled eggs, toasted hazelnuts and a honey mustard dressing.

Serves 4 as a lunch or starter

6 large leeks
2 large free-range eggs
  (at room temperature)
2 tbsp extra virgin olive oil
40g roasted hazelnuts,
  roughly chopped
Salt and freshly ground
  pepper

Vinaigrette
1 banana shallot, finely diced
1 garlic clove, finely grated
1 tsp Dijon mustard
1 tsp wholegrain mustard
1 tsp honey
3 tbsp white wine vinegar
5 tbsp extra virgin olive oil
2 tbsp flat-leaf parsley,
  finely chopped

1 If cooking on a barbecue, prepare and heat it up about 25 minutes before you intend to start cooking.

2 Trim the root ends of the leeks, cut off the dark green tops then wash the leeks thoroughly. Pat dry with kitchen paper.

3 Bring a small saucepan of water to the boil. Lower in the eggs and cook for 10 minutes to hard-boil. Drain and immerse the eggs in cold water to cool quickly. Lift them out and peel away the shells.

4 If using a large griddle pan, heat up over a high heat.

5 Drizzle the leeks with extra virgin olive oil and season well with salt and pepper. Place them on the barbecue or griddle pan and cook for 6–8 minutes until blackened all over, turning as necessary. Remove from the heat and set aside on a tray until cool enough to handle.

6 Meanwhile, make the vinaigrette. Whisk all the ingredients together in a bowl, seasoning with a little salt and pepper. Set aside until needed.

7 When the leeks are cool enough to handle, peel away and discard all the blackened skin. Halve the leeks lengthways and place, cut side up, on a serving platter.

8 Grate the hard-boiled eggs over the leeks and then spoon the vinaigrette over them. Sprinkle with the chopped hazelnuts to serve.

Broad bean, ricotta and lemon dip with flatbreads

Broad beans are a great summer vegetable (but it's also fine to use the frozen option). Ricotta gives this dreamy dip a lovely light, creamy texture and the minty, zesty flavours and whack of roasted garlic take it to another level. Making your own flatbreads to go with the dip is fun, too.

Serves 4 as a lunch or starter

Flatbreads
280g self-raising flour
250g natural yoghurt
2 tbsp extra virgin olive oil
1 tsp salt

Broad bean dip
500g freshly podded (or
   frozen) broad beans
1 preserved lemon, deseeded
   and roughly chopped
150ml extra virgin olive oil
200g ricotta
6 roasted garlic cloves
   (see page 176)
A handful of mint leaves, plus
   an extra few for the topping
Finely grated zest and juice
   of 1 lemon
Salt and freshly ground
   pepper

1. To make the flatbread dough, place all the ingredients in a large bowl and mix together to form a smooth dough. Tip out onto a lightly floured surface and knead well for a few minutes. Wipe out the bowl and place the dough back in it. Leave to rest for 30 minutes.

2. Meanwhile, bring a medium pan of water to the boil, add the broad beans and blanch for 2 minutes then drain and refresh in cold water. Gently squeeze the beans out of their skins.

3. For the broad bean dip, put 400g of the beans into a food processor; set aside the rest for the topping. Add the preserved lemon, 100ml extra virgin olive oil, the ricotta, roasted garlic and mint to the processor. Add the lemon zest and half the lemon juice and season well with salt and pepper. Blend until smooth, then spoon into a serving bowl.

4. In another bowl, mix the rest of the broad beans with the remaining lemon juice and extra virgin olive oil. Roughly tear a few mint leaves and add these, along with a little salt and pepper. Stir well and spoon over the broad bean dip.

5. To cook the flatbreads, heat up a griddle pan over a medium-high heat. Divide the dough into 4 even-sized pieces and shape into balls. Roll each one out thinly on a lightly floured surface to a round. Cook on the hot griddle, one at a time, for 1–2 minutes on each side. Keep warm, wrapped in a tea towel, while you cook the rest.

6. To serve, cut the warm flatbreads into wedges and place on a serving platter with the broad bean dip.

Chicory and pear Waldorf salad

This is my take on a classic Waldorf, with the slight bitterness of chicory balancing sweet pears and caramelised pecans beautifully. The salad is packed with bold flavours and contrasting textures, which complement each other well. If you can, opt for a local semi-soft blue cheese – I like to use Bath Blue.

Serves 4 as a lunch or starter

1 tbsp olive oil
3 baby red chicory bulbs,
    halved lengthways
100ml red wine
100ml chicken stock
1 small ripe pear
2 chicory bulbs, trimmed
    and leaves separated
2 handfuls of watercress,
    coarse stems removed
60g semi-soft blue cheese,
    such as Roquefort or
    Bath Blue, crumbled

Caramelised pecans
30g pecan nuts
1 tbsp icing sugar

Blue cheese dressing
50g semi-soft blue cheese,
    such as Roquefort or
    Bath Blue
1 banana shallot, finely diced
½ garlic clove, crushed
½ tsp Dijon mustard
1 tsp wholegrain mustard
1 tsp honey
2 tbsp white wine vinegar
4 tbsp extra virgin olive oil
1 tbsp finely chopped chives
Salt and freshly ground
    pepper

1   First, prepare the caramelised pecans. Preheat the oven to 200°C/180°C Fan/Gas 6 and line a baking sheet with baking paper.

2   Tip the pecans into a bowl, sprinkle over the icing sugar and mix well. Lay the sugared pecans out in a single layer on the lined tray. Place in the oven for 10 minutes or until well toasted and caramelised.

3   Next, make the dressing. Crumble the 50g blue cheese into a medium bowl, add 1 tbsp hot water and mash well. Add the shallot, garlic, both mustards, the honey and wine vinegar to the bowl and whisk well. Trickle in the extra virgin olive oil, whisking as you do so, until it is all incorporated. Season with salt and pepper to taste and stir in the chives.

4   For the salad, place a medium frying pan over a medium-high heat and add the olive oil. When hot, place the baby red chicory in the pan, cut side down, and cook for 2–3 minutes or until charred. Turn each chicory half over.

5   Pour the wine into the pan and let bubble until it is reduced by half. Add the stock and continue to cook until the liquid is evaporated and the chicory is tender. Remove the pan from the heat.

6   Halve the pear, remove the core and slice lengthways into fairly thick slices.

7   To assemble the salad, divide the seared baby chicory halves, fresh chicory leaves, watercress and pear slices between individual serving plates. Spoon over the blue cheese dressing and scatter over the crumbled blue cheese and caramelised pecans.

Pickled radish and sea bass crudo

Crudo means 'raw', and this dish is like a ceviche, where the acid in the citrus dressing effectively cooks the fish. However, the real stars of the show in this vibrant salad are the radishes, which take on a radiant hue once they are pickled. This is a great way to enjoy them.

Serves 4 as a starter or lunch

8 breakfast radishes
8 round red radishes
¼ daikon radish, peeled
¼ small beetroot, peeled
2 sea bass fillets (250g each),
 skin removed and pin-boned

Pickling liquor
300ml white wine vinegar
2 tsp yellow mustard seeds
1 star anise
120g golden caster sugar

Citrus dressing
Juice of 1 lime
Juice of ½ pink grapefruit
1 tsp white wine vinegar
3 tbsp extra virgin olive oil
1 tsp Dijon mustard
2 tsp finely chopped chives
Salt and freshly ground
 pepper

To finish
2 tbsp salad cress

1 First, prepare the pickling liquor. Pour the wine vinegar into a small saucepan and add the mustard seeds, star anise and sugar. Place over a medium heat and bring to a gentle simmer, stirring until the sugar is dissolved. Remove from the heat and leave to cool.

2 Halve the breakfast radishes lengthways and place in a small jar. Thinly slice 6 round radishes and add to the jar. Thinly slice the daikon radish and beetroot and place in a second jar. Pour the pickling liquor over these veg to cover. Leave for at least 2 hours, overnight if you have time.

3 Finely slice the other 2 round radishes on a mandoline and place in a bowl of iced water to crisp up.

4 Thinly slice the sea bass fillets, using a very sharp knife on an angle, into 5mm thick slices, and lay them flat on a tray.

5 For the citrus dressing, whisk all the ingredients together in a bowl until evenly blended. Spoon half of the dressing over the fish and leave to marinate in the fridge for 15 minutes.

6 When you are ready to serve, drain the pickled veg and the chilled radishes.

7 Lay the marinated sea bass slices on a serving platter and spoon over the remaining dressing. Scatter over the fresh radish slices and some of the pickled radish slices. Finish with the salad cress. Serve the remaining pickled radishes and beetroot on the side.

Peas with burrata and herb oil

Luckily for us, there are plenty of pea farmers on our east coast. In this dish, I combine cooked and raw peas, to appreciate their different qualities. Crispy Parma harm adds texture and the oozy burrata is sheer decadence. To enjoy the burrata at its best, take it out of the fridge around 30 minutes before eating.

Serves 2 as a lunch or starter

½ small sourdough baguette, thinly sliced
2 tbsp extra virgin olive oil
4 slices of Parma ham
250g freshly podded peas
1 tbsp white wine vinegar
2 burrata (125g each)

Herb oil
A small handful of mint leaves
A small handful of basil leaves
40ml extra virgin olive oil
80ml light olive oil
½ tsp caster sugar
Salt and freshly ground pepper

To finish
A small handful of pea shoots

1   Preheat the oven to 200°C/180°C Fan/Gas 6. Line an oven tray with baking paper.

2   Brush the sourdough slices on both sides with the extra virgin olive oil and sprinkle with a little salt. Place them on the lined tray and lay the Parma ham slices on the tray too. Pop the tray in the oven for 10 minutes or until the bread is golden and the Parma ham is crisp.

3   Meanwhile, prepare the herb oil. Have a bowl of iced water ready. Put the herbs into a heatproof bowl, pour boiling water over them and leave for 30 seconds, then drain and plunge into the iced water to cool quickly. Drain the herbs again and squeeze out excess moisture.

4   Pop the herbs into a small food processor (or nutribullet). Add the extra virgin and light olive oils, the sugar and some salt and pepper. Blend until smooth then strain the oil through a muslin-lined sieve into a jug or bowl; set aside.

5   Add 150g of the peas to a small pan of boiling salted water and simmer for 2 minutes or until tender. Drain and refresh in cold water, then drain again.

6   Mix the cooked peas with the raw peas, wine vinegar and 2 tbsp of the herb oil. Season with salt and pepper to taste.

7   Place a burrata on each serving plate and spoon the peas alongside. Drizzle with the herb oil and scatter over the pea shoots. Serve with the crispy Parma ham slices and sourdough toasts.

Spring greens and feta filo pie

In the UK, spring greens describe the 'first cabbage of the year'. They are the young, harvested plants that do not yet feature a tough interior core. In this satisfying spring greens pie, I also whack in cavolo, chard and plenty of cheese. The crisp, golden filo pastry topping provides the perfect textural contrast.

Serves 8

400g spring greens, shredded
200g cavolo nero, stalks
  removed and shredded
250g rainbow or Swiss chard,
  thinly sliced, including
  the stalks
1 tbsp extra virgin olive oil
40g butter
3 leeks, trimmed, washed
  and thickly sliced
  (350g prepared weight)
6 garlic cloves, thinly sliced
2 handfuls of mint leaves,
  roughly chopped
300g feta, crumbled
80g Parmesan, finely grated
Finely grated zest of 1 lemon
¼ nutmeg, finely grated
2 large free-range eggs,
  lightly beaten
Salt and freshly ground
  pepper

To assemble
100g butter, melted
270g packet filo pastry
30g sesame seeds

1 Preheat the oven to 200°C/180°C Fan/Gas 6.

2 Have ready a large bowl of iced water. Fill a very large saucepan with boiling water, place over a high heat and season heavily with salt. When the water comes back to the boil, add the spring greens, cavolo and chard and cook for 2 minutes or until they turn a vibrant green.

3 Drain the greens in a large colander in the sink and run cold water over them until they are cool enough to handle. Transfer the greens to the bowl of iced water and leave for 5 minutes or until cooled completely.

4 Meanwhile, put the extra virgin olive oil into a large sauté pan and place over a medium-high heat. Add the butter and when it is melted and foaming, toss in the leeks and garlic. Cook, stirring well, for 5 minutes or until the leeks are softened. Season well with salt and pepper and remove from the heat.

5 Drain the greens. Place half of them in a clean tea towel and squeeze out the excess water then transfer to a large bowl. Repeat with the rest of the greens. Add the softened leeks to the bowl, along with the mint, feta, Parmesan, lemon zest, nutmeg and beaten eggs. Stir everything together well and season with salt and pepper.

6 To assemble, brush the inside of a 26cm round shallow cast-iron ovenproof dish liberally with melted butter. Unravel the filo pastry sheets and cover them with a damp cloth to prevent them drying out. Take a sheet of filo, brush it evenly with butter and lay in the dish, leaving the excess overhanging the edges. Repeat with another 5 sheets of filo, making sure there is some overhanging around the outside.

7   Spoon the filling into the dish and smooth the surface flat with the back of a spoon. Cut the remaining filo in half so that you have 2 stacks of square pieces (rather than long rectangle sheets).

8   Brush half of the filo squares with butter and arrange them over the filling, tucking the edges in around the filling. Sprinkle with a layer of sesame seeds. Lift some of the overhanging pieces of filo and fold them over the top layer of filo. Repeat with the remaining filo, brushing with more butter and sprinkling over the remaining sesame seeds. Lastly, sprinkle with salt.

9   Place the pie in the oven on a lower shelf and cook for 30 minutes or until the filo is golden and crisp all over.

10   Remove the filo pie from the oven and cut into large wedges. Serve at once, with a crisp salad on the side if you fancy.

Pictured overleaf

Roasted cauliflower cheese

Cauliflower has been grown in the UK since the seventeenth century, and it was the classic cauli cheese bake that stole our hearts (and got our kids to eat veg). This version includes leek, which lends a sweet, oniony flavour, and a little curry powder for a flavour twist.

***Serves 4 as a main,
6 as a side***

1–2 large cauliflowers
(800g trimmed weight)
2 tbsp olive oil
½ tsp ground turmeric
1½ tsp medium curry powder
1 large leek, trimmed, washed
and thickly sliced
60g butter
60g plain flour
700ml whole milk
2 tsp English mustard
¼ nutmeg, finely grated
125g ball of mozzarella, torn
into large chunks
120g Cheddar, grated
80g Cherrywood Smoked
Cheddar (or Montgomery),
grated
50g sourdough breadcrumbs
Salt and freshly ground
pepper

1   Preheat the oven to 200°C/180°C Fan/Gas 6.

2   Divide the cauliflower into florets, saving the leafy stalks. Place the florets on an oven tray, drizzle with 1 tbsp olive oil and sprinkle with the turmeric, 1 tsp curry powder and a few pinches of salt. Mix well with your hands until the florets are evenly coated. Roast in the oven for 25 minutes or until the cauliflower is starting to brown.

3   Meanwhile, scatter the leek slices on a second tray, along with the cauliflower stalks. Drizzle with the remaining 1 tbsp olive oil and sprinkle with a little salt and pepper. Roast in the oven for 15 minutes or until the leek is softened.

4   To make the sauce, melt the butter in a saucepan over a medium heat and cook until it turns golden brown. Add the flour and cook, stirring with a wooden spoon, for 1 minute. Swap the spoon for a whisk and slowly add the milk, whisking constantly to keep the sauce smooth. Cook for 2–3 minutes or until thickened.

5   Turn the grill element on in the oven, keeping the oven setting the same. Add the mustard, remaining ½ tsp curry powder, the nutmeg, mozzarella and half of each of the grated cheeses to the sauce and stir until the cheese is melted. Season with salt and pepper to taste.

6   Place the roasted cauliflower, leek and cauli stalks in a large ovenproof dish. Mix well and then pour over the sauce. Scatter over the sourdough breadcrumbs and sprinkle with the remaining cheeses. Place on the middle shelf of the oven for 15–20 minutes until the sauce is bubbling and the topping is golden brown. Serve straight away.

Creamy kale pasta with crispy Parmesan

Kale is a hardy brassica that can be grown in most areas of the UK, and I often speak about how much I love its irony flavour. Here, I blitz it to make a creamy, nutritious pasta sauce. I think you will be suitably impressed with your crispy Parmesan garnish too!

Serves 2 as a main

60g Parmesan, finely grated
5 garlic cloves, peeled but
    left whole
175g de-stemmed kale leaves,
    roughly torn
250g dried mafalda (or other
    ribbon pasta) or spaghetti
80ml extra virgin olive oil
2 handfuls of basil leaves
100ml double cream
Finely grated zest of ½ lemon
    (optional)
Salt and freshly ground
    pepper

1   Preheat the oven to 200°C/180°C Fan/Gas 6. Line a baking tray with baking paper.

2   Take half of the Parmesan and place it in 4 equal piles on the lined tray. Pop the tray in the oven for 10–12 minutes or until the cheese is melted into 4 golden brown discs. Remove from the oven and set aside.

3   Bring a large saucepan of salted water to the boil. When boiling, add the garlic cloves and cook for 2 minutes then add the kale. Cook for a further 2–3 minutes and then scoop out the kale and garlic with a slotted spoon and transfer to a small food processor (or nutribullet).

4   Bring the water back to the boil then add the pasta and cook until *al dente* (cooked but still with a bite). Towards the end of cooking, scoop out 100ml of the pasta water and add it to the processor with the extra virgin olive oil, remaining Parmesan and the basil. Blitz until you have a smooth kale purée.

5   Pour the cream into a medium sauté pan and bring to a simmer over a medium-low heat. Drain the pasta as soon as it is cooked, saving a little of the water, and add to the pan with the kale purée. Stir well until the sauce is thickened and coats the pasta well. If you need to loosen the sauce, just add a little more pasta water. Add the lemon zest, if using, and season with pepper to taste.

6   Divide the creamy kale pasta between warmed bowls. Crumble over the crispy Parmesan and tuck in!

Charred hispi cabbage with sourdough crumb

I love sweet hispi cabbage, and I'm thrilled that it is in season all year. Here, I cook it simply: sauté to char the edges, simmer to tenderise and finish in a butter emulsion. However, I threw everything at the sourdough crumb – including salty anchovies, which complement the sweet cabbage beautifully.

Serves 4 as a side

2 medium hispi cabbage,
    outer leaves removed
2 tbsp rapeseed oil
200ml chicken stock
20g cold butter, cut into cubes
Salt and freshly ground
    pepper

Sourdough crumb
1 tbsp rapeseed oil
60g butter
2 banana shallots, halved
    lengthways and thinly sliced
2 garlic cloves, finely chopped
6 anchovies, roughly chopped
80g sourdough, crusts
    removed and blitzed to
    coarse crumbs
2 sprigs of rosemary, leaves
    picked and finely chopped
1 tbsp finely chopped flat-leaf
    parsley
Finely grated zest of 1 lemon

1   Quarter the cabbages lengthways. Heat the rapeseed oil in a very large non-stick sauté pan over a high heat. Season the cabbage wedges with a little salt and pepper and place in the pan, cut side down. Cook for 2–3 minutes on each side until the edges are nicely charred.

2   Remove from the heat and pour in the stock. Place the pan back on the heat and pop the lid on. Simmer for 8–10 minutes or until the cabbage is tender.

3   Meanwhile, prepare the sourdough crumb. Place a medium frying pan over a medium-high heat. Add the rapeseed oil and butter. When the butter is melted and begins to foam, add the shallots, garlic and anchovies. Cook for 2–3 minutes to soften the shallots.

4   Sprinkle the sourdough crumb over the shallot mix and cook, stirring regularly, for 3–4 minutes or until the crumbs start to turn golden brown. Add the chopped rosemary and cook for another 2 minutes, or until the crumbs are deep golden brown. Remove from the heat and stir through the chopped parsley. Set aside.

5   Remove the lid from the sauté pan of cabbage, drop in the butter cubes and swirl the pan to emulsify the butter into the sauce.

6   Transfer the cabbage to a warmed serving platter and sprinkle the sourdough crumb and lemon zest over the top. Serve at once.

Brussels sprouts with bacon and sage

For this recipe the Brussels sprouts are thinly sliced before cooking, so for those who haven't outgrown their dislike for them, there won't be a tiny cabbage in sight! The sweet-sharp dressing pairs well with the smoky bacon, and toasted hazelnuts and sage add interest too. A lovely side dish that makes an excellent accompaniment to your Christmas dinner.

Serves 4 as a side

1 tbsp rapeseed oil
30g butter
150g thick-cut smoked
    streaky bacon, cut into
    1cm strips
A large handful of sage leaves
1 large onion, finely sliced
600g Brussels sprouts, thinly
    sliced or shredded
2 tbsp honey
2 tbsp cider vinegar
30g toasted hazelnuts, halved
Salt and freshly ground
    pepper

1 Heat the rapeseed oil and half of the butter in a large frying pan over a medium-high heat until the butter is melted and foaming. Add the bacon and cook for 6–8 minutes until it is golden and starting to turn crisp.

2 Add the sage leaves to the pan and cook for a further minute. Remove the bacon and sage leaves from the pan with a slotted spoon and transfer to a plate; set aside.

3 Return the pan to the heat and add the remaining butter. When it is melted and foaming, add the onion and cook for about 6 minutes until softened.

4 Add the Brussels sprouts to the pan and cook, stirring often, for about 4 minutes until starting to wilt. Add the honey and cider vinegar and stir well. Season with salt and pepper to taste and remove the pan from the heat.

5 Transfer the sprouts to a warmed serving dish and scatter over the bacon and sage. Top with the toasted hazelnuts and serve straight away.

Tenderstem broccoli and feta traybake

This is an easy, attractive bang-in-the-oven traybake boasting all the flavours that remind us of summer. You will love the citrusy note the roasted lemon brings, as well as the bursting, roasted tomatoes – but it's the tenderstem broccoli that takes centre-stage with the intoxicating flavour it acquires once lightly charred.

Serves 4 as a main

200g sourdough
4 tbsp extra virgin olive oil,
    plus extra to finish if you like
1 garlic bulb, divided
    into cloves
2 blocks of feta (200g each),
    halved (to give 4 rectangles)
300g tenderstem broccoli
300g cherry tomatoes
    on-the-vine
1 lemon, thickly sliced
4 sprigs of oregano, leaves
    picked (optional)
80g kalamata olives
1 tsp Aleppo pepper flakes
2 tbsp sherry vinegar
Salt and freshly ground
    pepper

1   Preheat the oven to 200°C/180°C Fan/Gas 6.

2   Tear the sourdough into bite-sized pieces, spread out on a large oven tray and drizzle with 2 tbsp extra virgin olive oil. Add the garlic cloves to the tray and season with salt and pepper. Place in the oven for 10 minutes.

3   Take the tray from the oven and add the feta, broccoli, cherry tomatoes and lemon slices. Drizzle with the remaining 2 tbsp extra virgin olive oil and sprinkle with the oregano, if using. Season again with salt and pepper.

4   Place the tray back in the oven for 15–20 minutes. Ideally the broccoli should be slightly charred and the feta browned at the edges. (But you can always use a cook's blowtorch to get a little more colour on the feta.)

5   Remove the tray from the oven and scatter over the olives. Sprinkle the Aleppo pepper flakes over the feta and drizzle sherry vinegar over the whole tray. Add another drizzle of extra virgin olive oil if you like and serve on warmed plates.

Broccoli and sausage pasta

Broccoli is easy to grow in the UK and our farmers ensure we never run low. Most people enjoy the florets, but the stalks are fantastic, too. Here, I blend the stalks as part of a punchy pesto to dress the pasta. Chunks of Italian sausage turn it into a hearty main dish and the chilli butter is a great finish if you fancy a spicy kick.

Serves 4 as a main

1 large head of broccoli (500g)
400g dried pasta shells
2 large handfuls of
    basil leaves
50ml extra virgin olive oil
50g Parmesan, grated, plus
    extra to serve if you like
1 tbsp light olive oil
500g Italian pork sausages,
    skin removed
1 large onion, finely sliced
3 garlic cloves, sliced
Salt and freshly ground
    pepper

Chilli butter

80g butter
1 large long red chilli,
    thinly sliced

1   Bring a large saucepan of water to the boil. Cut the stalk from the broccoli and chop it roughly. Cut the head into small florets: you need about 320g florets. When the water is boiling, season it well with salt. Add the chopped broccoli stalk and cook for 2 minutes, then scoop out using a slotted spoon and place in a colander. Refresh under cold running water and drain. Transfer to a plate.

2   Add the broccoli florets to the boiling water and cook for 1–2 minutes. Scoop them out into the colander and run under cold water. Drain and set aside with the stalk.

3   Now add the pasta to the pan of boiling water and stir well. Cook until *al dente* (cooked but still with a bite). Drain in the colander, saving at least 300ml of the water. Run cold water over the pasta to cool it, drain and set aside.

4   Put the blanched broccoli stalk into a small food processor, along with a handful of the florets (100g), the basil, extra virgin olive oil, half the Parmesan and a good ladleful of pasta water. Blend to make a smooth pesto and season well with salt and pepper.

5   Place a large, wide pan over a medium-high heat and add the light olive oil. Break the sausage meat into pieces and add to the pan. Cook for around 4–5 minutes until the sausage meat starts to brown.

6   Add the onion to the pan and cook, stirring, for 2–3 minutes. Toss in the garlic, stir well and cook for another 2 minutes. Add the broccoli pesto, along with another ladleful of pasta water, and stir well.

7   Return the pasta to the pan, stir and heat for 3–4 minutes or until it is warmed though. Add the rest of the blanched broccoli florets and the remaining Parmesan, stir well and heat through for another 2–3 minutes.

8   Meanwhile, for a spicy finish, make the chilli butter. Heat the butter in a small pan until melted and foaming then add the chilli with a pinch of salt and cook for 1–2 minutes. Remove from the heat.

9   To serve, divide the broccoli and sausage pasta between warmed bowls and sprinkle over some extra Parmesan if you fancy. Spoon over the chilli butter for a spicy kick, and enjoy!

Pictured overleaf

Bacon and mushrooms eggs Benedict

Earthy, umami-rich mixed mushrooms add to the punchy decadence of this brunch, which is finished with a classic rich and buttery hollandaise. It is important to cook out the yolks to prevent your hollandaise sauce splitting.

Serves 2 as a lunch or brunch

Hollandaise
50ml white wine
100ml white wine vinegar
4 black peppercorns
1 banana shallot, chopped
2 sprigs of tarragon
2 large free-range egg yolks
25ml double cream
150g clarified butter
    (see page 23)
Lemon juice, to taste
Salt and freshly ground pepper

Sautéed mushrooms
1 tbsp olive oil
150g smoked bacon lardons
300g mixed mushrooms (such
    as King, pink and yellow
    oyster and shiitake), cut or
    torn into even-sized pieces
30g butter
2 garlic cloves, finely chopped
3 sprigs of thyme, leaves picked

Poached eggs
4 large free-range eggs (must
    be very fresh)
35ml white wine vinegar

To serve
4 English muffins, tops
    trimmed off
1 tbsp finely chopped chives

1   Put the wine, wine vinegar, peppercorns, shallot and tarragon into a small pan over a high heat. Let bubble until reduced to 2 tbsp liquid. Strain into a heatproof bowl, add the egg yolks, cream and 1 tbsp water and set over a pan of simmering water. Whisk constantly for 3–4 minutes or until frothy and thick (the texture of mayonnaise). Lift the bowl off the pan.

2   Slowly add a third of the clarified butter in a thin stream, whisking as you do so. Whisk in the remaining butter, then add salt, pepper and lemon juice to taste. Pass through a sieve into a bowl. If the hollandaise is too thick, whisk in a little warm water. Set aside in a warm place.

3   Heat the olive oil in a large non-stick frying pan over a high heat. Add the bacon lardons and cook for 5–8 minutes until crispy. Toss in the mushrooms and butter and sauté for 3–4 minutes. Add the garlic and thyme and cook for another 2 minutes. Season and take off the heat.

4   To poach the eggs, bring a pan of water to a simmer. Add 1 tsp wine vinegar to each of 4 small bowls and crack an egg into each. Leave for 1 minute (the vinegar helps to set the egg white). Add 1 tbsp wine vinegar and a good pinch of salt to the pan of simmering water. Carefully tip in each egg and poach very gently for 2–3 minutes, until the white is set but the yolk is still soft and runny.

5   Meanwhile, toast the muffins on both sides. Carefully lift the poached eggs from the pan using a slotted spoon and drain on a plate lined with kitchen paper. Place the bowl with the hollandaise back over the pan of simmering water to heat through, whisking gently.

6   Place 2 muffins on each plate and spoon on the sautéed bacon and mushrooms. Top each with a poached egg and spoon over the hollandaise. Sprinkle with chives to serve.

Beetroot, mint and bulgur wheat salad

There are so many ways to enjoy the earthy flavour of magnificent beetroot. If
you can get them fresh from the ground, there is a strong feeling of connection
with Mother Nature. Here, beets are roasted and served over nutty bulgur wheat.
Crumbled feta goes brilliantly with the beetroot (it's a classic pairing after all)
and the liberal use of fresh herbs gives the salad freshness and vibrancy.

Serves 4 as a lunch or starter

4 medium beetroot
  (600g in total)
1 tbsp olive oil
1 tbsp pomegranate molasses
400ml vegetable stock
200g bulgur wheat
A handful of dill leaves,
  roughly chopped
A handful of mint leaves,
  roughly chopped
A handful of flat-leaf parsley
  leaves, roughly chopped
100g feta, crumbled
Salt and freshly ground
  pepper

Dressing
3 tbsp olive oil
1 tsp Dijon mustard
2 tbsp red wine vinegar
1 tbsp pomegranate molasses

1   Preheat the oven to 200°C/180°C Fan/Gas 6.

2   Peel the beetroot and cut into wedges. Place on a small oven
    tray and drizzle with the olive oil and pomegranate molasses.
    Sprinkle with salt and pepper and roast in the oven for
    40 minutes or until the beetroot wedges are tender, turning
    them halfway through.

3   Meanwhile, heat the stock in a medium saucepan, tip in the
    bulgur wheat and stir well. Bring to a simmer, put the lid on
    the pan and cook for 5 minutes. Turn the heat off and leave
    to finish cooking in the residual heat for 15 minutes. Remove
    the lid and fork through the grains.

4   Tip the bulgur wheat into a large bowl and leave to cool down.
    Once cooled, add the chopped herbs and crumbled feta and
    fork through.

5   To make the dressing, put all the ingredients into a small
    bowl, season well with salt and pepper and whisk to
    combine. Pour the dressing over the bulgur wheat and mix
    well. Taste to check the seasoning and adjust as necessary.

6   Remove the roasted beetroot from the oven and leave to cool
    slightly, then toss half of it through the salad.

7   Spoon the bulgur wheat salad onto a platter and top with the
    remaining roasted beetroot to serve.

Kohlrabi remoulade, smoked salmon and rye bread

A remoulade traditionally calls for celeriac, but here I'm using kohlrabi for a change. Although it's not considered a root vegetable, it is robust enough to swap in, and quite delicious enjoyed crispy and raw. I love it with smoked salmon and rye bread, keeping true to a Scandinavian-influenced spread.

Serves 2 as a lunch or starter

1 medium kohlrabi
   (200g peeled weight)
1 green eating apple

Dressing
Juice of ½ lemon
1 tbsp white wine vinegar
1 tsp Dijon mustard
1 tsp wholegrain mustard
75g mayonnaise
50g soured cream
2 tbsp curly parsley,
   finely chopped
Salt and freshly ground
   pepper

To serve
4 slices of smoked salmon
4 slices of rye bread, toasted
Lemon wedges

1   Have ready a medium bowl of iced water. Cut the kohlrabi into julienne strips and immerse in the iced water. Halve and core the apple, cut into julienne strips and add to the iced water with the kohlrabi. Leave for 5–10 minutes; this will help keep them both crisp.

2   Meanwhile, to make the dressing, put all the ingredients into a large bowl, adding a good pinch each of salt and pepper, and whisk to combine.

3   Drain the kohlrabi and apple julienne and lay on a clean tea towel to dry, then add to the dressing and toss well.

4   Serve the kohlrabi remoulade with slices of smoked salmon, toasted rye bread and lemon wedges.

Turnip gratin with Lincolnshire Poacher

A farmer once described the turnip as 'not a sexy vegetable', but I think they can be! Here, I've included turnip in a classic potato bake to enhance the flavour with its unique peppery notes, and added thyme and garlic for extra flavour. Of course, the golden cheese topping is irresistible.

Serves 6 as a side

1 tbsp softened butter,
  to grease the dish
600ml double cream
3 garlic cloves, finely grated
4 sprigs of thyme, leaves
  picked
600g Maris Piper potatoes
600g turnips
85g Lincolnshire Poacher,
  grated
Salt and white pepper

1 Preheat the oven to 150°C/130°C Fan/Gas 2. Lightly grease a 20 x 30cm oven dish, 7cm deep, with butter.

2 Pour the cream into a small saucepan and add the garlic and thyme. Stir well and place over a medium-low heat. Season the cream generously with salt and white pepper and heat very gently for around 10 minutes.

3 Meanwhile, peel and thinly slice the potatoes and turnips, using a mandoline if you have one.

4 Layer a third of the potatoes and turnips in the oven dish, overlapping them slightly as you go. Pour over a third of the warm cream. Add another layer of potatoes and turnips, then half of the remaining cream. Repeat the layers once more. Bake in the oven for 20 minutes.

5 Take the dish out of the oven and push the potato and turnip slices down with a fish slice. (This encourages the release of starches in the veg to help thicken the sauce.) Put the gratin back in the oven and bake for a further 30 minutes, repeating the pressing down process every 10 minutes.

6 Increase the oven setting to 220°C/200°C Fan/Gas 7 and turn the grill element on.

7 Remove the dish from the oven and scatter the grated cheese over the gratin. Place back in the oven on a higher shelf for a final 20 minutes or until golden brown on top and tender when you insert a skewer through the middle. Remove from the oven and leave to stand for 5 minutes before serving.

Honey roast parsnips

Parsnips are among my favourite vegetables. They boast a natural sweetness and are easy to prepare. To truly celebrate them, I'm serving sweet and sticky roasted parsnips on a rich and creamy, curry-flavoured purée made from... you guessed it... parsnips. Just brilliant!

Serves 4 as a side

600g parsnips
3 tbsp olive oil
3 tbsp honey
3 sprigs of rosemary, leaves
    picked and finely chopped
Salt and freshly ground
    pepper

Parsnip purée
300g parsnips
1 tbsp olive oil
30g butter
1 onion, chopped
1 tsp curry powder
300ml chicken stock
200ml double cream

1   Preheat the oven to 200°C/180°C Fan/Gas 6 and line a large tray with baking paper.

2   Peel the parsnips and halve or quarter lengthways, depending on size. Lay them on the lined tray. In a small bowl, mix the olive oil, honey and chopped rosemary together and season generously with salt and pepper. Pour this mixture over the parsnips and toss well to ensure they are all evenly coated. Roast in the oven for 20 minutes.

3   Meanwhile, make the parsnip purée. Peel the parsnips and cut into even-sized chunks. Place a medium saucepan over a medium-high heat and add the olive oil and butter. When the butter is melted and foaming, add the onion and cook for 5 minutes to soften. Add the curry powder and cook, stirring, for 1 minute. Now add the parsnip chunks and stock. Bring to a gentle simmer and cook for 20 minutes or until the parsnips are tender.

4   After 20 minutes, take the tray of parsnips out of the oven, stir them around and roast for another 20–25 minutes or until golden and caramelised.

5   When the parsnips for the purée are tender, add the cream to the pan and stir well. Bring back to a simmer and cook for 10 minutes or until thickened. Remove from the heat and season with salt and pepper to taste. Transfer the contents of the pan to a jug blender and blitz until smooth.

6   Spoon the parsnip purée onto a warmed serving dish and top with the roasted parsnips to serve.

Swede and beef Cornish pasties

I am not trying to improve on what a good-quality shop-bought Cornish pasty offers, but there is something deeply satisfying about making your own. Here, I'm including the traditional tasty swede, but the essential thing to remember is that the raw filling steam-cooks within the pastry, so it must be sealed well.

Serves 4 as a main

Pastry
465g plain flour, plus extra
　to dust
1 tsp fine salt
100g cold lard, diced
100g cold butter, diced
1 large free-range egg, beaten
　with 1 tsp water, to glaze

Filling
1 large onion, finely sliced
200g swede (peeled weight),
　cut into 1cm cubes
100g potato (peeled weight),
　cut into 1cm cubes
300g skirt steak, cut into
　2cm cubes
3 sprigs of thyme, leaves
　picked
60g salted butter, thickly
　sliced
Salt and white pepper

1　To make the pastry, sift the flour and salt into a large bowl. Add the lard and butter and rub in with your fingertips until the mixture resembles breadcrumbs. Make a well in the centre and slowly pour in 100ml ice-cold water, stirring as you do so with the handle of a wooden spoon, to combine.

2　Transfer the dough to a lightly floured surface and knead briefly until smooth. Wrap in cling film and leave to rest in the fridge for 1 hour.

3　Preheat the oven to 200°C/180°C Fan/Gas 6 and line an oven tray with baking paper.

4　To make the filling, mix all the ingredients except the butter together in a bowl, seasoning generously with salt and white pepper.

5　Divide the dough into 4 equal portions. Dust a surface lightly with flour and roll each piece out to a 20cm circle. Spoon a quarter of the filling onto one half of each pastry round, leaving a 2cm border around the edge. Dot the sliced butter evenly over the filling.

6　Brush the pastry edges with egg glaze. Fold the pastry over the filling and press the edges together to seal. To crimp the edge of each pasty, press down on one corner with your finger and press the adjacent pastry inwards with the forefinger of your other hand. Continue to fold over and pinch the pastry to form a crimped edge.

7　Brush each pasty all over with egg glaze and place on the lined tray. Sprinkle each one with a little sea salt. Bake on the middle shelf of the oven for 40–45 minutes or until golden brown. Serve warm from the oven.

Celeriac soup

Celeriac is a stunning root vegetable and pairing it with apple in a soup is an idea I've shared often in the past. While it's tricky to improve on earlier versions, the mighty-flavoured sage butter with toasted walnuts will have you remembering this version for a long time.

Serves 4 a lunch or starter

3 tbsp rapeseed oil
2 leeks, halved lengthways
   and thickly sliced
2 garlic cloves, sliced
1 Bramley apple, peeled
   and diced
1 large parsnip, peeled
   and diced
800g peeled celeriac
   (prepared weight), cut
   into 2.5cm pieces
3 sprigs of thyme, tied
   together
1.2 litres chicken or
   vegetable stock
150ml double cream
150ml crème fraîche
Salt and freshly ground
   pepper

Walnut and sage butter

80g butter
40g walnuts, roughly chopped
20 sage leaves

To serve

Thick slices of sourdough,
   toasted

1 Heat the rapeseed oil in a large non-stick saucepan over a medium heat. Add the leeks and garlic and cook gently for 8 minutes or until softened but without any colour.

2 Add the apple, parsnip, celeriac, thyme and stock. Bring to a simmer and put the lid on. Reduce the heat slightly and cook for about 20 minutes or until the veg are soft. Remove and discard the thyme bunch.

3 Using a jug blender, blitz the soup in batches until smooth. Return the soup to the pan and place over a gentle heat. If it is a little thin, simmer for a few more minutes; if it's too thick, add a splash more water.

4 Taste the soup and season with salt and pepper. Stir in the cream and crème fraîche and keep warm.

5 For the walnut and sage butter, melt the butter in a small saucepan over a high heat. When it begins to brown, stir in the chopped walnuts and sage leaves. Cook for 1 minute and then remove the pan from the heat.

6 Ladle the soup into warmed bowls and trickle the walnut and sage butter over the top. Serve with the toasted sourdough on the side.

Ricotta and herb potato bake

I want to give centre-stage to the humble spud because the UK happens to be one of the world's largest producers of potatoes. Ricotta keeps this potato bake deliciously creamy and there are massive flavours from the garlic, nutmeg and herbs. There is also a respectful nod to my beloved Gloucester cheese.

Serves 6 as a side, 4 as a lunch

1 tbsp softened butter,
  to grease
1.5kg waxy potatoes (Red
  Rooster or Maris Piper)
300ml single cream
200ml whole milk
4 sprigs of thyme, leaves
  picked
2 small garlic cloves,
  finely grated
¼ nutmeg, finely grated
250g ricotta
Finely grated zest of 1 lemon
2 tbsp roughly chopped dill
2 tbsp finely chopped chives
100g Double Gloucester,
  grated
2 tbsp finely chopped
  flat-leaf parsley (optional)
Salt and freshly ground
  pepper

1   Preheat the oven to 180°C/160°C Fan/Gas 4. Grease an oven dish, 20 x 30cm and 7cm deep, with butter. Peel and thinly slice the potatoes, using a mandoline if you have one.

2   Pour the cream and milk into a small saucepan. Add the thyme, garlic and nutmeg and season generously with salt and pepper. Bring to a gentle simmer over a medium heat.

3   Meanwhile, in a bowl, mix the ricotta with the lemon zest, dill, chives and some salt and pepper.

4   Layer a third of the potatoes in the oven dish, overlapping them slightly as you go. Pour over half of the warm cream mix. Spoon on half of the ricotta mix then add another layer of potatoes. Pour over the rest of the cream mix and spoon on the remaining ricotta. Top with a final layer of potatoes. Cover the dish with foil and bake in the oven for 40 minutes.

5   Take the dish out and turn the oven setting up to 220°C/200°C Fan/Gas 7.

6   Remove the foil and sprinkle the grated cheese evenly over the surface. Return the dish to the oven, uncovered, for 15–20 minutes or until the cheese is golden and bubbling.

7   Remove from the oven and leave to stand for 5 minutes before serving, sprinkled with chopped parsley if you like.

Layered 'chips'

Maris Piper potatoes have been growing in the UK since the swinging sixties and they are ideal to use in this fun spin on chips. While the method may seem a bit involved, it will be worth your love and effort. The accompanying dip, however, takes seconds to throw together and is simply perfect!

Serves 6–8 as a side or snack

100g duck fat
100g butter
3 sprigs of thyme
3 sprigs of rosemary
2.5kg Maris Piper potatoes
1 tsp Maldon sea salt, plus
    extra to season
½ tsp white pepper
Vegetable oil, to fry

To serve
150ml soured cream
2 tbsp chopped chives
A few spoonfuls of caviar
    (optional)

1   Preheat the oven to 170°C/150°C Fan/Gas 3. Line a 23cm square baking tin with baking paper. Have another similar-sized baking tin to hand.

2   Put the duck fat, butter, thyme and rosemary into a small saucepan and place over a medium-low heat. Heat very gently for 5 minutes then take the pan off the heat and leave to infuse for 10 minutes.

3   Meanwhile, peel and thinly slice the potatoes, using a mandoline if you have one. Trim the rounded edges, so the slices can be positioned flush to the baking tin.

4   Strain the infused mixture through a sieve into a bowl and season with the salt and pepper.

5   Layer the potato slices in the lined tin, brushing each layer liberally with the infused mix. Cover the top layer with baking paper and sit the other baking tin on top.

6   Bake in the oven for about 2 hours until the potatoes are completely tender (test with a cocktail stick). Leave to cool and then weigh down the top tin with a few weights or tins. Refrigerate overnight.

7   The next day, turn out the potato bake onto a board. Trim the edges, then cut into 16–20 'chips'. Heat a 2cm depth of oil in a large non-stick frying pan over a medium-high heat. When hot, fry the chips, turning until golden brown and crisp on all sides. Drain on kitchen paper.

8   Season the soured cream with a little salt and pepper. Sprinkle the chips with salt and serve with the soured cream, a scattering of chives and some caviar if you fancy!

Fish & Shellfish

As an island nation, we're literally surrounded by the most incredible fish and seafood. Sadly though, we don't tend to cook a lot of it at home in Britain today. We'll eat it when we're on holiday or when we're dining out. Most people have childhood memories of sitting on a beach, eating fish and chips wrapped in paper and slathered in salt and vinegar, while it's blowing a gale.

But as much as this is up there as one of the best British food experiences, fish and seafood deserve so much more than this. Different areas of the coast are home to different varieties of fish and seafood. In the cold North Atlantic, you'll find cod and haddock; closer to land the seas are home to shellfish like crabs, mussels, oysters and clams.

Scottish salmon is famous for its amazing quality, and although salmon farming has got a bit of a bad rap, done well it's actually a brilliant and sustainable way of producing the fish we buy most often here in Britain. Salmon is an easy fish to cook: you don't need to worry about it drying out as much and it can take some bold flavours. I've chosen to pan-fry it with Cajun spices (on page 94).

Even though fish comes from all over Britain – and there are certain seasons when they will be in their prime – you'll be able to buy fresh fish wherever you are, all year round.

> If you're lucky enough to live by the coast and can get your hands on freshly caught fish, straight from the boats, you'll know how incredible it tastes.

If you are unable to source locally caught fish, you'll find most fish is available fairly inexpensively from your local supermarket. If you buy your fish from a local fishmonger, what you need to look for is a really firm looking fish, with clear eyes and no sign of a strong fishy smell. Always feel free to ask your fishmonger to fillet fish for you too – anything to make it easier at home. The main thing to consider when cooking fish and seafood is understanding the texture. Oily fish like salmon, trout, mackerel and sardines are probably the easiest to start with as they are robust, hold their shape and retain their moisture well.

I'm a huge fan of sardines and mackerel – I love the simplicity of them. Sardines, quickly grilled or fried, have the most fantastic flavour; try my play on tinned sardines on toast (on page 102), while the smoky flavour of blow-torched mackerel contrasts brilliantly with the acidity of cucumber and cream (on page 100).

Meaty white fish like sea bass, haddock and cod are also hard to get wrong. Poached haddock kedgeree is very forgiving and packed with flavour – try my version on page 109, which uses smoked haddock. Smoking is a preserving process we're very good at in Britain and, as well as adding great flavour, it increases how long the fish will keep.

Cockles and mussels are relatively cheap and quick to cook, and are absolute powerhouses of flavour that work well with other bold ingredients like garlic, herbs and spices.

I love that you're able to make something as hearty and robust as my Cockle chowder on page 90 from something so cheap and plentiful. And on page 80 I've steamed Scottish mussels very simply in beer, with a touch of curry powder, fresh dill and parsley.

All of the recipes in this chapter are uncomplicated, use native fish and seafood you can source easily and, most importantly, celebrate their individual qualities.

If you're still feeling unsure about cooking with fish, start off by making the beer battered cod fingers on page 104; they're familiar, reassuring and tasty – stick them in a sandwich and you'll know exactly where you are.

Scallops with a creamy white wine sauce

Scallops are a sustainable bivalve, hand-picked by divers off the UK coastline. They are tender, sweet morsels that require very little effort when it comes to cooking. Here, I serve them with a creamy potato mash and thyme-flavoured wine sauce. The salty samphire adds a special touch to this light meal.

Serves 4 as a starter

4 extra-large hand-dived scallops, cleaned, in their half-shell
300g Maris Piper potatoes, peeled and diced
110g butter
1 banana shallot, finely diced
2 garlic cloves, finely chopped
2 sprigs of thyme, leaves picked
150ml white wine
200ml double cream
Juice of ½ lemon
1 tbsp olive oil
1 tbsp finely chopped parsley
Salt and freshly ground pepper
Steamed or blanched samphire, to finish

1   Using a sharp knife, lightly score the white scallop meat in a criss-cross pattern, season with salt and pepper and set aside. Clean the half-shells thoroughly.

2   Put the potatoes into a small saucepan, cover with water and season with salt. Bring to a simmer over a high heat, lower the heat and cook for 8–10 minutes or until the potatoes are tender. Drain and pass through a potato ricer into another pan (or use a potato masher to mash them).

3   Return the empty pan to a medium heat, add 80g of the butter and stir until melted. Add the shallot and sauté for 4–5 minutes or until softened. Add the garlic and thyme and cook for another 2 minutes.

4   Pour in the wine, turn the heat up and let bubble until it is reduced by half. Now add the cream and simmer gently for 4–5 minutes or until thickened. Remove from the heat, stir in the lemon juice and season with salt and pepper.

5   Add half of this creamy sauce to the mashed potato, stir through and place over a gentle heat to warm through.

6   Meanwhile, place a small frying pan over a high heat and add the olive oil and remaining 30g butter. When the butter is melted and foaming, place the scallops in the pan and cook for 1–2 minutes on each side.

7   Divide the mash between the scallop shells. Stir the chopped parsley into the remaining sauce and spoon over the mash. Top each with a scallop and finish with a little steamed or blanched samphire.

Scottish mussels cooked in beer

The super-cold Scottish waters provide an excellent environment for molluscs to thrive, resulting in meaty, full-flavoured mussels. Scottish mussels are available at most fresh fish counters and they are easy to cook if you're up for it. The creamy sauce is flavoured with fennel, leek and garlic, plus a hint of curry powder, for a winning combination. I often cook mussels in ale or white wine, but I reached for Scottish beer here, which works brilliantly.

Serves 2

1kg Scottish mussels in
   their shells
300ml Scottish beer
50g butter
1 tbsp olive oil
1 leek, trimmed, washed,
   halved lengthways
   and sliced
2 garlic cloves, finely chopped
2 celery sticks, finely diced
¼ fennel bulb, finely diced
1 tsp mild curry powder
200ml double cream
3 tbsp crème fraîche
Salt and freshly ground
   pepper

Parsley oil
2 handfuls of flat-leaf
   parsley leaves
100ml light olive oil

To serve
2 slices of brown sourdough,
   toasted
Triple-cooked chips
   (page 105), optional

1 Wash the mussels in a colander under cold running water and de-beard them. Place a large saucepan (that has a tight-fitting lid) over a high heat to heat up.

2 Add the mussels to the hot pan, pour in the beer and put the lid on. Steam over a medium-high heat for 6–8 minutes until the mussels are opened; discard any that stay closed.

3 Meanwhile, prepare the parsley oil. Bring a small pan of water to the boil and have a bowl of ice-cold water ready. Drop the parsley leaves into the boiling water for 30 seconds, then drain and immerse the parsley in the cold water to refresh. Drain again and squeeze out any excess water.

4 Pop the parsley leaves into a small food processor (or nutribullet). Add the olive oil and a little salt and blend until smooth. Strain the oil through a muslin-lined sieve into a jug or bowl; set aside.

5 Drain the mussels in a muslin-lined colander over a bowl to strain and collect the liquor to use later on.

6 Put the saucepan back over a medium heat and add the butter with the 1 tbsp olive oil. Once melted, add the leek and cook for a few minutes until starting to soften. Add the garlic, celery and fennel and cook for a further 2–3 minutes. Sprinkle in the curry powder and cook, stirring frequently, for 1–2 minutes.

7 Pour the reserved mussel cooking liquor onto the vegetables and let bubble until it is reduced by half. Add the cream and crème fraîche and simmer for another 5 minutes or until the sauce is lightly thickened.

8   Add the mussels back to the pan and stir until they are well coated in the sauce. Warm through for a few minutes then remove from the heat. Taste to check the seasoning and adjust as necessary.

9   Spoon the mussels and sauce into warmed shallow bowls and drizzle with the parsley oil. Serve with the toasted sourdough alongside for mopping up the delicious sauce. Enjoy – with a plate of chips on the side if you fancy!

Pictured overleaf

Crab cakes

We get succulent fresh crab from Cornwall and Orkney, but store-bought picked crab meat is a convenient way to enjoy this tasty shellfish. I add smoked paprika to these easy crab cakes, which lends a distinctive flavour not often used with seafood. The accompanying mayo – flavoured with fragrant dill, sharp lemon and salty capers – is a lovely foil.

Makes 12

400g cod fillet, skin removed
   and pin-boned
1 large free-range egg white
1 tsp Dijon mustard
Finely grated zest of 1 lemon
¼ tsp white pepper
½ tsp smoked paprika
200g white crab meat
1 tbsp finely chopped chives
1 tbsp roughly chopped dill
50g panko breadcrumbs
Vegetable oil, to fry
Salt and freshly ground
   pepper

Caper mayonnaise
150ml good-quality
   mayonnaise
Juice of ½ lemon
3 tbsp baby capers
2 tsp finely chopped dill

To serve
Lemon wedges

1 Cut the cod into large chunks and place in a small food processor. Add the egg white, mustard, lemon zest, white pepper and smoked paprika. Blend until smooth.

2 Transfer the fish mixture to a bowl. Add the crab meat and chopped herbs with a good pinch of salt and fold through until the mixture is well combined.

3 Tip the panko breadcrumbs into a shallow bowl. Wet your hands with a little water (to avoid sticking) then divide the fish mixture into 12 even-sized pieces and shape into patties.

4 Place each patty in the breadcrumbs and turn to coat well on both sides. Place these crab cakes on a tray in the fridge for 20 minutes to firm up.

5 Meanwhile, for the caper mayonnaise, put all the ingredients into a small bowl and mix well, seasoning with a little salt and pepper.

6 Heat about a 1cm depth of oil in a large non-stick frying pan over a medium-high heat. When it is hot, carefully add the crab cakes and cook for 2–3 minutes on each side or until golden brown and cooked through. Remove from the pan and drain on a tray lined with kitchen paper.

7 Season the crab cakes with a little salt and serve them on individual plates with a dollop of caper mayonnaise and a lemon wedge.

Oysters two ways

There are many ways to enjoy British oysters apart from raw with a squeeze of lemon. Here are a couple of ideas, including one for those who don't like the idea of eating these delicacies uncooked. To stop the oyster shells moving around on the plate, sit them on little mounds of dampened sea salt flakes.

Makes 24

2 dozen oysters, cleaned
  and opened

Pickled cucumber and apple
75g peeled and deseeded
  cucumber (prepared weight)
½ tsp salt
120ml cider vinegar
1½ tbsp caster sugar
50g peeled, quartered and
  cored Granny Smith apple
  (prepared weight)
2 tsp finely chopped dill

Bacon sauce
1 tbsp olive oil
30g butter
2 thick slices of smoked
  back bacon (100g in total),
  finely diced
2 banana shallots, finely diced
3 garlic cloves, finely chopped
2 tbsp good-quality barbecue
  sauce
2 tbsp Worcestershire sauce
1 tbsp tomato ketchup

To finish
2 tbsp salmon roe caviar

1. For the pickle, finely dice the cucumber, place in a small bowl and sprinkle with the salt. Pour the cider vinegar into a small pan, add the sugar and place over a low heat. Stir until the sugar is dissolved. Remove from the heat and leave to cool.

2. Pour the cooled liquid over the cucumber and leave to pickle for 15 minutes. Finely dice the apple, add to the cucumber and stir well. Place in the fridge until needed.

3. To prepare the bacon sauce, heat the olive oil and butter in a small frying pan over a medium-high heat. When the butter is melted and foaming, add the bacon and cook for 3–4 minutes until starting to caramelise. Add the shallots and garlic and cook for 3–4 minutes until softened. Take off the heat and stir in the barbecue and Worcestershire sauces, and the tomato ketchup.

4. Preheat the oven to 200°C/180°C Fan/Gas 6 with the grill element on.

5. Lay 12 oysters on an oven tray and spoon 1 tbsp of the bacon sauce over each one. Place on a medium-high shelf under the grill for around 5–8 minutes until the oysters are cooked through and the sauce is bubbling.

6. Meanwhile, arrange the other 12 fresh oysters on 2 large serving plates. Stir the chopped dill through the cucumber pickle and then spoon it over the fresh oysters, adding some of the pickling liquid. Top with a few caviar pearls.

7. Transfer the cooked oysters to another 2 serving plates and serve alongside the raw oysters.

Steamed razor clams with sherry and fennel

Razor clams are usually available all year round and there are several species found in British waters. They make an attractive meal and, like all molluscs, cook quickly. Here they are steamed and enhanced with the lovely flavours of fennel and sherry, then finished with a bacon crumb to add texture.

Serves 4

1kg razor clams
2 tbsp rapeseed oil
1 banana shallot, finely diced
2 garlic cloves, finely chopped
150g fennel, finely diced
1 long red chilli, deseeded and
    finely diced
150ml dry sherry
150ml fish or chicken stock
30g cold butter, cut into cubes
Salt and freshly ground
    pepper

Bacon crumb

4 thick rashers of smoked
    streaky bacon (90g in total),
    finely diced
30g butter
30g sourdough breadcrumbs
1 tbsp finely chopped
    flat-leaf parsley

1   Rinse the razor clams thoroughly under cold running water to remove the sand from their shells.

2   For the bacon crumb, put the bacon into a medium frying pan and place over a medium-high heat for 3–4 minutes or until the fat starts to render. Add the butter and let it melt. Once the bacon starts to crisp up, add the sourdough crumbs and stir well. Cook for 3–4 minutes or until the crumb is golden brown and crisp. Tip into a bowl and set aside to cool. Once cooled, stir through the chopped parsley.

3   Wipe out the frying pan with kitchen paper, place back over a medium-high heat and add the rapeseed oil. When it is hot, toss in the shallot and garlic and sauté for 2–3 minutes. Add the fennel and cook for a further 3–4 minutes. Now add the chilli and cook for 1 minute. Remove the pan from the heat.

4   Place a large sauté pan (that has a tight-fitting lid) over a high heat to heat up. Add the razor clams to the hot pan with the sherry and stock. Put the lid on and steam for 4–5 minutes or until the clams open. Take off the heat. When cool enough to handle, remove and discard one half of each shell. Strain the liquor through a muslin-lined sieve into a bowl.

5   Place the veg pan back on the heat and pour in the clam cooking liquor. Bring to a gentle simmer, add the butter and stir to emulsify. Now add the razor clams to the pan and warm through briefly. Taste to check the seasoning.

6   Transfer the clams and veg to a warmed serving platter and sprinkle over the bacon crumb to serve.

Cockle chowder

Cockles are bountiful in the West Country and their method of cooking is the same as mussels. In this comforting chowder, I celebrate sweet, Welsh cockles with the classic combo of garlic, cream and smoked bacon. If you are feeling a little lazy and want to avoid preparing cockles, you can use 285g frozen prepared cockle meat and omit the cockles-in-shell garnish.

Serves 4

2kg cockles
250ml white wine
A handful of parsley stalks
4 garlic cloves: 2 smashed;
    2 sliced
60g butter
150g smoked streaky bacon,
    cut into 1cm strips
1 large white onion, diced
1 leek, trimmed, washed,
    halved lengthways and
    thickly sliced
3 celery stalks, diced
1 bay leaf
3 sprigs of thyme
2 heaped tbsp plain flour
200ml whole milk
300g potatoes, peeled and
    cut into 1cm dice
150ml double cream
2 tbsp crème fraîche
2 tbsp finely chopped flat-leaf
    parsley
Salt and white pepper
1 tbsp rapeseed oil, to finish
1–2 tbsp finely chopped
    chives, to garnish
Crusty bread, to serve

1   Wash the cockles thoroughly under cold running water then soak in a bowl of well-salted cold water for at least an hour to remove the sand from their shells. Rinse again.

2   Place a large saucepan (that has a tight-fitting lid) over a high heat to heat up. Add the cockles to the hot pan with the wine, parsley stalks, smashed garlic cloves and 500ml water. Put the lid on and cook for 4–5 minutes until the cockle shells are opened; discard any that stay closed.

3   Drain the cockles through a muslin-lined colander over a bowl to strain and collect the liquor to use later on. Leave until cool enough to handle, then set aside 16–20 cockles to serve. Remove the rest of the cockles from their shells.

4   Wipe out the pan with some kitchen paper and place back over a medium-high heat. Add the butter to the pan. Once it is melted, toss in the bacon strips and cook, stirring often, for 5–6 minutes or until crispy. Add the onion and sauté for 3–4 minutes. Now add the leek, celery, sliced garlic, bay leaf and thyme and cook, stirring occasionally, for 2 minutes.

5   Sprinkle in the flour and cook, stirring, for 2–3 minutes. Gradually stir in the reserved cockle cooking liquor, keeping the mixture smooth. Stir in the milk, a little at a time, and bring to a gentle simmer.

6   Add the potatoes and cook for 8–10 minutes or until they are tender. Using a potato masher, gently mash some of the potatoes in the pan to help thicken the soup. Now stir in the cream and crème fraîche and simmer gently for 3–4 minutes or until the soup thickens a little more.

7   Add the shelled cockles to the pan to warm through and season with salt and white pepper. Add the chopped parsley and stir through.

8   Ladle the cockle chowder into warmed bowls and top each serving with a few cockles in their shells. Drizzle with a little rapeseed oil, scatter over the chopped chives and serve with crusty bread on the side.

Pictured overleaf

Salmon with Cajun spices

This is my kind of food. There isn't much you won't love about this exciting meal where a Cajun spice does all the punchy flavour work for you. The salmon fillets are seasoned with it, and so is the accompanying creamy sauce. If you can, opt for Scottish salmon.

Serves 2

2 salmon fillets (280g each),
   skin on
2 tsp Cajun spice blend
1–2 tbsp olive oil
30g butter

Cajun crème fraîche sauce
1 tbsp olive oil
2 banana shallots, finely diced
2 garlic cloves, finely diced
½ tsp Cajun spice blend
150ml fish stock
150ml crème fraîche
Juice of 1 lemon, or to taste
1 tbsp finely chopped flat-leaf
   parsley
Salt and freshly ground
   pepper

To serve
Lemon wedges

1   Score the skin of the salmon with a sharp knife. Sprinkle both sides of the fillets with the Cajun spice mix and a little salt. Put the olive oil into a medium non-stick frying pan and place over a medium heat.

2   When the oil is hot, add the salmon to the pan, skin side down, and press each fillet down with a fish slice for a few seconds. Cook for 3–4 minutes on each side then take the pan off the heat.

3   Add the butter to the pan and, as it melts, baste the salmon with it. Transfer the salmon to a warmed plate and leave to rest in a warm place while you make the sauce.

4   Place the frying pan back over a medium-high heat and add the olive oil. Toss in the shallots and cook for 3 minutes or until starting to soften. Add the garlic and Cajun spice blend and cook, stirring, for another 2 minutes.

5   Add the stock to the pan and let it bubble to reduce by half. Now stir in the crème fraîche and cook for a minute or two until the sauce thickens. Season with salt and pepper and add lemon juice to taste. Remove from the heat and stir through the chopped parsley.

6   Spoon the creamy sauce onto warmed serving plates and top with the salmon. Serve with lemon wedges and accompany with tenderstem broccoli or green beans.

Rainbow trout with citrus butter sauce

Rainbow trout is sadly underused despite being a brilliant, sustainable British fish. Ask your fishmonger to help you prep it, leaving you to focus only on the fun task of cooking it. My accompanying citrus butter is a beautiful finish that won't take away from the clean, mild flavour of the fish.

Serves 2

2 rainbow trout, heads
  removed, gutted and
  cleaned
2 tbsp olive oil
1 lemon, thinly sliced
Salt and freshly ground
  pepper

Citrus butter sauce

1 tbsp olive oil
1 banana shallot, finely
  chopped
Juice of ½ lemon
Juice of ½ pink grapefruit
Juice of ½ orange
100g cold butter, cut into
  cubes
1 tbsp finely chopped chives
1 tbsp finely chopped dill

To serve

1 tbsp olive oil
100g mangetout
100g sugar snap peas

1   Preheat the oven to 220°C/200°C Fan/Gas 7. Line an oven tray with baking paper.

2   Place the trout on the lined tray, season both sides with salt and pepper and drizzle with the olive oil. Stuff the fish cavities with the lemon slices. Place in the oven and bake for 15 minutes.

3   Meanwhile, make the sauce. Heat the olive oil in a medium saucepan over a medium heat, add the shallot and sauté for 3–4 minutes or until softened. Add the citrus juices to the pan and let bubble for 2 minutes. Now whisk in the butter, a few pieces at a time, until fully incorporated. Remove from the heat and season with salt and pepper to taste. Set aside; keep warm.

4   Heat the olive oil in a saucepan over a medium heat. Add the mangetout and sugar snap peas along with 2 tbsp water and some salt and pepper. Cook for 2–3 minutes until just tender then remove from the heat.

5   When the trout is cooked, take the tray from the oven. Leave until the fish is cool enough to handle, then peel the skin away from both sides.

6   Transfer the trout to warmed serving plates. Stir the chopped herbs through the citrus butter sauce and then spoon it over the fish. Serve the mangetout and sugar snaps alongside.

Red mullet with fennel, chorizo and chickpeas

Caught near to the shore on the southwest coast of England, red mullet is a delicate fish which boasts a high fat content. Its unique texture is celebrated in this simple dish, where, despite all the other big flavours, it remains the star of the show.

Serves 2

4 small red mullet fillets, pin-boned
2 tbsp rapeseed oil
100g cooking chorizo, diced
1 shallot, diced
100g fennel, diced
1 small courgette (100g), diced
½ tsp smoked paprika
1 tbsp tomato purée
250ml chicken or fish stock
400g tin chickpeas, drained
30g butter, melted
Finely grated zest and juice of ½ lemon
1 tbsp roughly chopped dill
Salt and freshly ground pepper

1 Preheat the oven to 190°C/170°C Fan/Gas 5 with the grill element on. Season the red mullet fillets on both sides with salt and pepper and set aside.

2 Heat 1 tbsp rapeseed oil in a sauté pan over a medium-high heat, add the chorizo and cook until crispy. Remove with a slotted spoon and set aside.

3 Place the pan back over the heat. Add the shallot and cook for 2–3 minutes or until softened. Toss in the fennel and sauté for 2 minutes. Add the courgette, smoked paprika and tomato purée and stir over the heat for 2 minutes.

4 Pour in the stock and bring to a simmer. Add the chickpeas, bring back to a simmer and lower the heat. Simmer very gently for 15 minutes or until the veg are tender and the liquid is reduced by half.

5 Lay the red mullet fillets skin side up on an oven tray and brush with melted butter. Place on a high shelf in the oven for 5 minutes or until cooked through.

6 Return the crispy chorizo to the sauté pan and add the lemon zest and juice. Stir and warm through, adding the chopped dill and seasoning with salt and pepper to taste.

7 Divide the chorizo and veg between 2 shallow serving bowls. Top each portion with 2 red mullet fillets and serve.

Mackerel with pickled cucumber and blinis

Mackerel has a powerful, distinctive flavour and is an inexpensive fish that remains in good supply here in Britain. My favourite way to cook this fatty fish is simply to fire up the blowtorch and crisp the skin. Here it is enjoyed with sharp pickled cucumber, a creamy mustard dip and homemade blinis.

Serves 2

4 mackerel fillets
1 tbsp extra virgin olive oil
Salt and freshly ground
   pepper

Pickled cucumber
½ cucumber, peeled and
   thinly sliced
150ml cider vinegar
150ml apple juice
1 tsp coriander seeds
1 tsp fennel seeds
1 tsp Maldon sea salt
1 tsp sugar
1 tbsp roughly chopped dill

Mustard crème fraîche
120ml crème fraîche
1 tsp wholegrain mustard
1 tsp honey

Blinis
100g plain spelt flour
1 tsp baking powder
1 large free-range egg,
   separated
125ml buttermilk
20g butter, melted, plus an
   extra 20g to cook

To serve
Lemon wedges

1   For the pickled cucumber, place the cucumber in a heatproof bowl. Put the cider vinegar, apple juice, coriander and fennel seeds, salt and sugar into a saucepan and bring to the boil, stirring. Remove from the heat and let cool slightly. Strain the pickling liquor and pour over the cucumber. Leave to pickle for 1 hour.

2   For the mustard crème fraîche, mix all the ingredients together in a bowl and season with salt and pepper to taste; set aside.

3   To make the blini batter, stir the spelt flour and baking powder together in a small bowl. Make a well in the middle and add the egg yolk, buttermilk and melted butter. Whisk until smooth.

4   In a clean bowl, whisk the egg white until stiff peaks form. Add the egg white to the batter, with a little salt and pepper, and fold in gently until just combined.

5   Place a large non-stick frying pan over a medium heat and add the 20g butter. When it is melted and foaming, spoon in heaped tablespoonfuls of the batter, spacing them apart, to make about 8 thick blinis.

6   Oil the mackerel fillets all over with the extra virgin olive oil and season with salt and pepper. Run a cook's blowtorch over both sides of the fillets to cook them.

7   Drain the pickled cucumber and toss through the chopped dill. Arrange 2 mackerel fillets and 4 blinis on each plate with a portion of pickled cucumber and a dish of mustard crème fraîche alongside. Serve with lemon wedges.

Sardines on toast

Let's move on from tinned sardines because fresh sardines are a real treat when they're in season. I enjoyed these sardines direct from the boat, and with the harbour winds blowing, it felt truly special to be eating something straight from the sea. With its lovely companions, this is next-level sardines on toast.

Serves 4

4 thick slices of sourdough
2 tbsp extra virgin olive oil,
　plus extra to drizzle
12 butterflied sardines
3 large ripe tomatoes,
　thickly sliced
Salt and freshly ground
　pepper

Pickled red onion

1 medium red onion, peeled
　and thinly sliced
1 tbsp caster sugar
4 tbsp red wine vinegar or
　sherry vinegar
2 tbsp roughly chopped
　flat-leaf parsley

Fennel salad (optional)

2 fennel bulbs, trimmed
　and cut lengthways into
　3cm-thick slices
1½ tbsp olive oil
1 garlic clove, grated
1 small preserved lemon, peel
　only, roughly chopped
Juice of 1 lemon
2 tbsp pitted green olives,
　roughly chopped
1 tbsp finely chopped dill
1 tbsp finely chopped chives

1　First prepare the pickled red onion. Put the onion into a small heatproof bowl, cover with boiling water and leave to stand for 10 minutes. Drain the onion and return to the bowl. Add the sugar and vinegar and stir well. Season with salt and pepper. Leave the onion to pickle for at least 20 minutes.

2　If you are cooking on a barbecue, prepare and heat up about 25 minutes before you intend to start cooking. If using a griddle pan, heat up over a high heat about 5 minutes ahead.

3　To make the salad, if serving, brush the fennel slices with olive oil and cook on the barbecue or griddle for 3–5 minutes each side until golden brown and charred. Remove and let cool slightly then cut into small chunks. Mix the remaining olive oil, garlic, preserved lemon and lemon juice together in a bowl to make a dressing. Add the olives, fennel and chopped herbs, toss to mix and season with salt and pepper to taste.

4　Brush the sourdough slices with the extra virgin olive oil on both sides. Barbecue or griddle over a high heat for 2–3 minutes on each side until golden and charred.

5　In the meantime, season the butterflied sardines with salt and pepper and brush with extra virgin olive oil. Cook on the griddle or on a perforated barbecue tray (or directly on the grid) for 1–2 minutes on each side. Drain the pickled red onion, add the chopped parsley and toss through.

6　Place the toasted sourdough on warmed plates. Lay a few tomato slices on each toast slice and season with salt and pepper. Spoon the fennel salad, if serving, over the tomatoes.

7　Arrange 3 sardines on top of each serving and finish with a few pickled red onion slices and a final trickle of extra virgin olive oil. Serve straight away.

Beer battered cod, tartare sauce and mushy peas

Fish 'n' chips is so utterly British and loved by all! I've put a little twist on the nation's favourite by serving the fish goujon-style. These beer-battered cod pieces are served with classic mushy peas and a homemade tartare sauce. Don't skip that all-important squeeze of lemon to finish.

Serves 4

4 skinless cod fillets (about
   150g each), pin-boned
Vegetable oil, to fry
Salt and freshly ground
   pepper

Beer batter
1 egg white
225ml beer or sparkling water
150g self-raising white flour
½ tsp bicarbonate of soda

Tartare sauce
200ml good-quality
   mayonnaise
1 banana shallot, finely diced
1 tsp Dijon mustard
40g gherkins, finely diced
2 tbsp baby capers, finely
   chopped
2 tbsp finely chopped flat-leaf
   parsley
2 tbsp finely chopped dill
Juice of ½ lemon

Mushy peas
100ml chicken stock
350g frozen peas
2 tbsp roughly chopped
   mint leaves
1 tsp white wine vinegar

1. Cut each cod fillet cut into 3 strips and season with salt and pepper; set aside.

2. To make the batter, put the egg white and beer or sparkling water into a bowl and beat, using a hand-held electric whisk, until fluffy. Add the flour, bicarbonate of soda and a pinch of salt and beat until smooth, to make a fairly thin batter, the consistency of double cream.

3. Cover the bowl and place in the fridge to rest the batter, while you prepare the tartare sauce and mushy peas.

4. To prepare the tartare sauce, put the mayonnaise into a bowl and add all the rest of the ingredients. Stir together until evenly combined and season with salt and pepper to taste; set aside.

5. For the mushy peas, bring the stock to a simmer in a small saucepan. Add the peas, bring back to a simmer and cook for 2–3 minutes or until just tender. Remove from the heat and add the chopped mint and wine vinegar. Transfer this mixture to a mini food processor and pulse until well blitzed but retaining a bit of texture. Scrape the mushy pea mixture back into the saucepan and pop the lid on to keep it warm.

6. Preheat the oven to 180°C/160°C Fan/Gas 4 and set a large wire rack over a baking tray. Heat a 5–7cm depth of oil in a large saucepan or deep sauté pan over a high heat to 170–180°C (check with a thermometer).

7. You will need to fry the pieces of fish in batches (to avoid lowering the temperature of the oil). Dip 6 pieces of fish into the batter and then carefully lower them into the hot oil.

8 Drizzle some extra batter over the fish pieces as they cook, if you like those extra crispy bits of batter. After 3 minutes, turn the fish over and cook until golden on the other side.

9 Lift the fish pieces out of the pan with a slotted spoon onto the wire rack. Season with salt. Scoop out any excess bits of batter from the oil. Place the tray in the oven to keep warm while you cook the remaining fish in the same way.

10 When you are ready to serve, heat up the mushy peas a little. Plate up your crunchy cod fingers. Serve with chips, tartare sauce, mushy peas and lemon wedges alongside.

Triple-cooked chips

1 Peel 4 large potatoes (for chipping) and cut into chips, about 1.5cm thick, then rinse under cold water to wash off some of the starch. Add the chips to a large pan of boiling water, bring back to the boil and boil for 5 minutes. Drain and spread out on a wire rack to dry and cool.

2 Heat your oil for deep-frying in a deep-fryer over a medium-high heat to 140°C. Lower the chips into the hot oil in a wire basket and deep-fry for 8–10 minutes. Remove and place on a wire rack to drain and cool until needed.

3 When ready to serve, heat the oil to 180°C and deep-fry the chips for about 4–5 minutes until golden and crispy. Remove and drain on kitchen paper. Season with salt.

Pictured overleaf

Smoked haddock kedgeree

Haddock is a wild-caught fish, cooked fresh or traditionally smoked in the UK. Smoked haddock provides the key flavour in a comforting, familiar kedgeree. In this version, a humble bowl of eggs, fish and rice is pimped a little by adding ingredients like coconut, curry, coriander and chilli for a somewhat exotic twist. A rich and robust dish, kedgeree is often enjoyed by Scottish fisherman before they head out to sea.

Serves 4

500ml fish stock
A pinch of saffron strands
500g smoked haddock fillet (skin on)
1 tbsp olive oil
50g butter
1 tsp black mustard seeds
1 tsp cumin seeds
8 curry leaves, roughly chopped
2 tsp mild roasted curry powder
320g basmati rice
80ml coconut cream
4 large free-range eggs
150g frozen peas, thawed
2 tbsp roughly chopped coriander (optional)
Salt and freshly ground pepper
1 red chilli, thinly sliced, to finish

1   Pour the stock into a small saucepan, add the saffron and bring to a low simmer. Lay the smoked haddock in the pan and pop the lid on. Simmer very gently for 5 minutes or until the fish is just cooked. Lift the fish out, using a fish slice, place on a tray and remove the skin; save the stock.

2   Heat the olive oil and butter in a sauté pan over a medium-high heat. When the butter is melted and foaming, add the mustard and cumin seeds and the curry leaves. Stir well over the heat for 1–2 minutes. Add the curry powder and cook, stirring, for another minute.

3   Tip the rice into the pan. Stir over the heat for a minute, then pour in the reserved stock and add some salt and pepper. Bring to a simmer, stir in the coconut cream, lower the heat and pop the lid on. Cook for about 15 minutes.

4   Meanwhile, bring a small pan of water to the boil and have a bowl of iced water ready. Lower the eggs into the pan and cook for 7 minutes, then lift out and immerse in the iced water. Remove the eggs, peel and halve or quarter them lengthways – the yolks should be squidgy, not runny.

5   When the rice is cooked, remove the pan from the heat, stir through the peas and replace the lid. Leave to stand for 5 minutes.

6   Flake the poached smoked haddock over the rice, add the chopped coriander, if using, and gently fork through.

7   Divide the kedgeree between warmed serving bowls and top each serving with the halved or quartered boiled eggs. Finish with a scattering of chilli slices.

Sea bass baked in a salt crust

The technique of baking fish in a salt crust is something you should try at least once as it results in seasoned moist flesh. I use sea bass here, which is a fantastic round white fish with a delicate flavour. This is also a great opportunity to use wild garlic when it's in season.

Serves 4

2 large sea bass fillets with
   skin (about 300g each)
6–8 large Swiss chard leaves,
   stems removed
3 large free-range egg whites
1 tbsp fennel seeds, lightly
   crushed
1.2kg coarse salt
1 lemon, thinly sliced
Salt and freshly ground
   pepper

1   Preheat the oven to 220°C/200°C Fan/Gas 7. Line a baking tray with baking paper. Check the sea bass fillets for pin bones, prising out any you find with tweezers.

2   Bring a large saucepan of salted water to the boil then add the chard leaves and blanch for 1 minute to soften. Drain the leaves in a colander and refresh under cold water then drain thoroughly.

3   Whisk the egg whites in a clean bowl until they form soft peaks, then stir through the fennel seeds and coarse salt. Spread a third of the salt mixture over the lined baking tray and flatten it out with your hands to create a bed for the fish.

4   Season the fish fillets with salt and pepper. Place one fillet skin side down on a board and lay the lemon slices on top. Place the other fillet, skin side up, on top. Now wrap the fish in the blanched chard leaves to enclose completely.

5   Lay the wrapped fish on the salt bed and cover with the rest of the salt mix, using your hands to mould it around the fish so that it is completely enclosed.

6   Bake in the oven for 30 minutes then remove the tray from the oven and leave the fish to rest for 5 minutes.

7   To serve, carefully crack open the salt crust and discard it. Slice the chard-wrapped fish into portions and transfer to warmed plates. Serve at once, with fried potatoes and a green salad on the side.

Dover sole with brown butter and capers

Dover sole has a unique flavour that even non-fish eaters often enjoy. It takes patience to prepare, but your fishmonger can help if you're not up for the challenge. Lemon sole is a more affordable alternative. Don't be deceived by the simple sauce – its whack of flavour will have you remembering it for a long time.

Serves 2

2 Dover sole (500–600g each)
50g plain flour
2 tbsp olive oil
Salt and freshly ground
   pepper

Brown butter and caper sauce
75g butter
Juice of 1 lemon
2 tbsp baby capers
1 tbsp flat-leaf parsley leaves,
   finely chopped

To serve
Lemon wedges

1   To prepare the fish, make a small cut around the gut cavity, which is located just below the head and pectoral fin, and pull out the guts and liver; rinse the cavity. Cut off all the fins with scissors and trim the tail. Using a large sharp knife, remove the head.

2   Make a small slit just above the tail with a sharp knife then use the tip of the knife to loosen a 1cm flap of skin that you can grip on to. Add a pinch of salt to the cut area. Now, holding the tail with one hand, pull the skin off towards the head. Repeat on the other side.

3   Now season both sides of the fish generously with salt and pepper. Season the flour as well, then sprinkle over both sides of the fish, to coat thoroughly – this will create a lovely crust on the fish after cooking.

4   Heat a large frying pan over a medium-high heat and add the olive oil. When hot, carefully lay each fish in the pan. Cook for 4–5 minutes on each side or until a golden crust forms.

5   Meanwhile, make the brown butter sauce. Melt the butter in a small saucepan over a medium-high heat. Continue to cook until the butter turns a rich golden brown and starts to release a nutty aroma. Remove from the heat and add the lemon juice to the pan; this will stop the cooking process. Add the capers and season with a little salt and pepper.

6   When the fish are cooked, transfer to warmed serving plates. Gently heat the brown butter sauce, stir in the chopped parsley and spoon over the fish. Add the lemon wedges and serve, with steamed asparagus (or another seasonal green veg) and new potatoes.

Halibut with yuzu beurre blanc

This uncomplicated dish features halibut: a flat white fish with a luxurious flavour. It is served with a classic creamy white wine sauce jazzed up with a little yuzu juice, which adds a sweet and zesty note. The whole lot is finished with brown shrimps because I love the strong, robust flavour these bring.

Serves 2

2 halibut fillets (200g each),
   skin on
1 tbsp light olive oil
80g shrimps
Salt and freshly ground
   pepper

Yuzu beurre blanc
1 banana shallot, finely diced
150ml white wine
150ml fish stock
2 tsp white wine vinegar
50ml double cream
100g cold unsalted butter,
   diced
1 tbsp yuzu juice
1 tbsp flat-leaf parsley leaves,
   finely chopped

1   First make the beurre blanc. Put the shallot, wine, stock and wine vinegar into a small saucepan. Bring to a simmer over a high heat and let bubble until reduced to 2–3 tbsp liquid.

2   Add the cream, stir well and continue to simmer until the liquor is reduced by half. Strain through a fine sieve into a jug and pour back into the pan. Set aside; keep warm.

3   Place the pan over a medium heat and whisk in the butter, a little at a time, until it is all incorporated. Stir in the yuzu and season with salt and pepper to taste.

4   Season both sides of the fish with salt and pepper. Heat the olive oil in a large non-stick frying pan over a medium-high heat. When the pan is hot, add the halibut fillets, skin side down, and cook without moving for 5 minutes.

5   Now flip the fish fillets over onto the flesh side and add the shrimps to the pan. Cook for 2 minutes and then remove the pan from the heat. Leave the fish to rest for a few minutes.

6   Add the chopped parsley to the beurre blanc and stir well. Gently peel the skin off the halibut. Transfer the fillets to warmed serving plates or bowls and spoon the shrimps on top. Pour the sauce over the fish and serve, with tenderstem broccoli on the side.

Meat & Poultry

Welcome to my favourite section of the book! It'll come as no surprise that this is the chapter that I'm most excited about. It's where I always want to be as a chef. I love the whole process involved in cooking with meat – from the butchery and prep work, through to the cooking methodology, and also that you can utilise the whole animal, right up to making delicious stocks and sauces from the bones.

We are world renowned for our British meat, and the quality speaks for itself. It's the climate that makes it so incredible – all that rain means lots of grass for cows and sheep to graze on.

How and where they're reared – the terroir – also has a huge impact on the flavour of the meat. Salt marsh lamb, for example, is sweet and very tender, while the hardworking Herdwick lamb, which scrambles over the mountains of the Lake District, is texturally different and tastes much gamier.

Grass-fed livestock is a much less intensive farming practice than grain-fed methods, making it more sustainable with less impact on the environment too. It's actually a very beautiful cyclical process – cows and sheep maintain and fertilise the ground, while the farmers tend to their animals, often for several years. These nurturing methods are part of our history in Britain, and I think those skills and expertise need to be nurtured and protected too. I've noticed a lot more care and consideration given to how we're all preparing and cooking meat in recent years.

There's been a shift away from traditional premium cuts towards cuts like beef shin, pork belly and short ribs. In turn, this has raised the quality and standard of our cooking because we've had to learn a whole new range of skills to get the best from these more complex cuts, which are often tougher and thicker.

We're also looking further abroad, borrowing cooking methods, flavours and ingredients from around the world and combining them with produce closer to home. We are braising, curing, American smoking and applying barbecuing techniques, as well as rubs and marinades to drive in even more flavour.

It's easy to impress with a premium cut, but it takes more work, more inventiveness to make mince feel special – and that's where those flavour enhancers come in as well: a little blue cheese in the smashed burgers on page 140, gentle spices in the lamb-stuffed tomatoes on page 153 and lemon and herbs in the meatballs on page 122.

In the lamb neck curry on page 150, for example, a slightly fattier cut is braised a little more slowly, enhanced with aromatic Indian spices. The bavette steak sandwich on page 138 is one of my favourites in this chapter. Bavette used to be known as the 'butcher's cut' as it was relatively cheap but high in flavour, owing to the fat marbling. You need to cook it nice and pink and slice it against the grain.

It is tricks like this which show an understanding of the structure of meat, and what different cuts require to celebrate their unique qualities.

But let's not forget the humble chicken! Appearing at least once on most people's midweek dinner tables, it's now such a staple it's lost some of its status and I think this is a real shame. Chicken is a fantastic meat to work with. You can make a lot of impact with as little as a simple flavoured butter or glaze – try the Honey and mustard chicken supremes (page 162) or Sticky sesame chicken wings (page 166).

Or opt for my go-to roast chicken on page 158, served with roast potatoes and salad, and dressed with the pan juices. Roast dinner is probably one of our nation's best exports and while this version is a change from a classic Sunday lunch with all the trimmings, it really highlights the flavours and textures of the whole bird.

Barbecued pork tomahawk steak

Up your game at the next barbecue by indulging in British tomahawk pork steaks! The spice mix used complements the meat, and the creamy sauce adds the perfect tang. When cooking fatty pork, always score the rind so the seasoning penetrates the meat: this will also result in a delightful, crispy fat edge.

Serves 4

2 tomahawk pork chops
   (about 650g each)
2 tbsp light olive oil
3 tsp paprika
3 tsp dried oregano
3 tsp garlic powder
Salt and freshly ground
   pepper

Paprika sauce

1 tbsp light olive oil
2 banana shallots, finely
   chopped
2 garlic cloves, finely chopped
1 tsp sweet smoked paprika
1 tsp paprika
1 tbsp tomato purée
150ml chicken stock
100ml double cream
2 tbsp crème fraîche

1. Prepare your barbecue, keeping a section free of coals, so you can cook the pork using indirect heat at times, as well as directly over the flames. Heat up the barbecue about 25 minutes before you intend to start cooking.

2. Using a small, sharp knife, score the rind of the pork chops at 1cm intervals. Brush the meat on both sides with olive oil. Mix the paprika, oregano and garlic powder with 1 tsp salt and a grinding of pepper. Sprinkle over the meat.

3. To make the paprika sauce, heat a frying pan over a medium heat and add the olive oil. When hot, add the shallots and cook for 3–4 minutes to soften. Toss in the garlic and cook for 2 minutes. Add both paprikas and the tomato purée and stir for 1 minute.

4. Now stir in the stock and let bubble until reduced by half. Stir in the cream and cook until the sauce thickens. Take off the heat and stir in the crème fraîche. Season with salt and pepper to taste. Set aside, ready to warm through to serve.

5. Place the pork chops on the barbecue over the coals and cook for 1–2 minutes, turning them as they get a good sear and colour. Once coloured all over, move the chops to the coal-free section to finish cooking over indirect heat, turning occasionally. The whole process should take around 18–20 minutes. The chops are ready when a digital probe thermometer inserted into the thickest part of the meat registers 65°C. Transfer them to a tray or plate to rest.

6. To serve, gently reheat the sauce and pour into a serving bowl. Cut the bone off each of the pork chops and slice the meat thickly. Arrange on a serving platter and serve the paprika sauce alongside for dipping. I like to barbecue some tenderstem broccoli to serve alongside this dish too.

Zesty pork and sage meatballs

Every country has its own unique twist on meatballs – whether it's in the mince mixture or in the sauce. In this easy dinner, I opt for British pork mince which is flavoured with aromatic sage, zesty lemon and salty anchovies. There are also sharp bursts of flavour in the accompanying caper sauce.

Serves 4

500g pork mince
20g fresh breadcrumbs
2 tbsp finely chopped sage
Finely grated zest of 1 lemon
3 anchovies, finely chopped
2 tbsp whole milk
30g plain flour, to coat, plus
    an extra 1 tbsp for the sauce
2 tbsp light olive oil
40g cold butter, cut into cubes
150ml white wine
200ml chicken stock
1 tbsp chopped flat-leaf
    parsley
1 tbsp baby capers
Salt and freshly ground
    pepper

1 To prepare the meatballs, put the pork mince, breadcrumbs, sage, lemon zest, anchovies and milk into a large bowl and season well with salt and pepper. Mix well with your hands for a few minutes until thoroughly combined.

2 Divide the pork mixture into 16 even-sized pieces and shape into balls. Put the meatballs onto a tray and place in the fridge to firm up for 15 minutes.

3 Tip the 30g flour onto a plate and roll the meatballs in it to coat well. Place a large non-stick sauté pan over a medium-high heat. When it is hot, add the olive oil, then the meatballs and cook, turning, until well browned all over. Remove them from the pan with a slotted spoon and set aside on a plate.

4 Toss half of the butter into the pan and stir until melted. Add the 1 tbsp flour and cook, stirring, for 1 minute. Pour in the wine and whisk until smooth then gradually whisk in the stock. Cook, stirring, until slightly thickened. Now whisk in the remaining butter cubes to emulsify and enrich the sauce.

5 Add the meatballs back to the pan and warm through in the sauce for 2–3 minutes. Season the sauce with salt and pepper to taste and stir through the chopped parsley and capers. Serve on warmed plates with mashed potato and rainbow chard or other greens.

Braised pork jowls with gremolata

We should be cooking nose-to-tail more often because cuts like pig jowls are inexpensive. If cooked right, this underused part of a pig's cheek can yield a stunning texture. I reach for the unique flavour of sherry vinegar in this recipe, but it's the dynamite gremolata that will have you smiling.

Serves 4

4 pork jowls (Bath chap style)
1 onion, roughly chopped
1 large carrot, roughly
  chopped
2 celery sticks, diced
2 garlic cloves, roughly
  chopped
2 tbsp sherry vinegar
1 tbsp tomato purée
3 sprigs of thyme
800ml chicken stock
2 tsp Dijon mustard
Salt and freshly ground
  pepper

Gremolata
50g sourdough, roughly torn
  into pieces
1 tbsp extra virgin olive oil
30g butter
2 anchovies
Finely grated zest of 1 lemon
2 tbsp finely chopped parsley

1   Trim off all the sinew from the pork jowls then season them well with salt and pepper. Place a wide heavy-based pan over a medium-high heat and add the pork jowls, fat side down (to render the fat) and cook for 4–5 minutes until golden brown.

2   Turn the pork jowls over and cook for 4–5 minutes until golden brown on the other side. Remove from the pan and transfer to a plate; set aside. Remove and discard all but 4 tbsp of the pork fat from the pan.

3   Now add the onion, carrot and celery to the pan and sauté for 6–8 minutes until they begin to soften. Toss in the garlic and cook for another minute. Now add half of the sherry vinegar and stir until bubbled away. Stir in the tomato purée and cook for a couple of minutes then add the thyme, pour in the stock and bring to a simmer.

4   Return the pork jowls to the pan and give the mixture another stir. Make sure the liquid covers the meat; if necessary top up with a little water. Place a cartouche (round of baking paper with a small hole cut in the centre) on the surface. Partially cover the pan with a lid and turn the heat to low. Simmer very gently for 1½ hours or until the meat is tender. (Alternatively, you can cook this in an ovenproof pan in a preheated oven at 180°C/160°C Fan/Gas 4.)

5   When the meat is tender, remove the jowls from the pan and set aside on a plate. Strain the sauce through a fine sieve into a clean saucepan, pressing the veg in the sieve to extract all the juice. Now add the remaining 1 tbsp sherry vinegar. Bring to a simmer and cook until slightly reduced and thickened.

6   Meanwhile, make the gremolata. Blitz the sourdough in a blender to crumbs. Heat the extra virgin olive oil and butter in a small frying pan. When the butter is melted and foaming, add the anchovies and stir well to break them down.

7   Add the sourdough crumbs to the pan and cook, stirring, until evenly golden brown. Take off the heat and season with salt and pepper to taste. Stir through the lemon zest and chopped parsley.

8   To serve, return the pork jowls to the sauce to warm through. Lift them out onto a board, brush each one with a little mustard and sprinkle generously with the gremolata. Spoon the sauce into warmed serving bowls and add a pork jowl to each portion. Serve with creamy mashed potato alongside.

Pictured overleaf

Roast pork belly with fennel and apple slaw

The UK boasts a high welfare standard when it comes to how our pigs are cared for and you can taste the love our farmers put in. I particularly love pork belly with its perfect meat to fat ratio. Here, it is served with a slaw that includes all the components that pair so beautifully with pork.

Serves 6–8

3kg pork belly, bone in,
  rind scored
2 tbsp fennel seeds
Flaky sea salt and freshly
  ground black pepper

Fennel and apple slaw
2 fennel bulbs, trimmed
2 Granny Smith apples,
  quartered and cored
2 Braeburn apples,
  quartered and cored
Juice of 1 lemon
2 tbsp roughly chopped
  tarragon leaves
2 tbsp roughly chopped
  flat-leaf parsley
2 tbsp roughly chopped dill
1 tsp Dijon mustard
1 tsp wholegrain mustard
100g crème fraîche
3 tbsp mayonnaise
2 tbsp cider vinegar

1   Lay the pork belly, skin side up, on a tray. Rub the skin with 2 tbsp sea salt, making sure you get it between the slits of the scored skin (to draw moisture from the fat, which helps the skin to crisp up). Leave for at least an hour, or in the fridge overnight if you have the time.

2   The next day, pat the pork skin dry with kitchen paper. Lightly crush the fennel seeds, using a pestle and mortar, and rub into the pork fat slits. Season the underside with pepper. Preheat the oven to 180°C/160°C Fan/Gas 4.

3   Put the pork, skin side up, on a wire rack. Sit the rack over a large roasting tin and pour 800ml water into the tin (not over the meat). Place on the middle shelf of the oven and roast for 2½–3 hours, rotating the tin halfway through and adding more water to the tin if necessary to prevent the underside of the pork from drying out.

4   Take out the pork and turn the oven up to 220°C/200°C Fan/Gas 7. When the oven is at this temperature, pop the pork back in on a high shelf and roast for another 35–45 minutes or until the crackling is puffed, crisp and golden.

5   Meanwhile, for the slaw, cut the fennel and apples into fine julienne and immerse in a bowl of iced water for 15 minutes to crisp up. For the dressing, mix the rest of the ingredients together in a large bowl. Drain the fennel and apple, pat dry with a clean tea towel and add to the dressing. Toss to combine and season with salt and pepper to taste.

6   Take the pork from the oven and leave to rest in a warm place for 10-15 minutes. Remove the bones from the underside then cut the pork into thick slices. Arrange on a warmed platter and serve with the slaw alongside.

Sausages with swede mash and onion gravy

It's hard to improve on a great pub classic (and a British family favourite). Here
I take bangers and mash up a notch by adding swede to the mash, which lends
a sweet, earthy flavour. I then smother the whole lot in a rich red wine and onion
gravy flavoured with thyme that makes the sausages sing!

Serves 4

1 tbsp vegetable oil
8 good-quality pork and herb
    sausages

Swede and black pepper mash
500g swede, peeled and cut
    into 1cm dice
500g Desirée potatoes, peeled
    and cut into 2.5cm chunks
80g butter
1 garlic clove, grated
2 sprigs of thyme, leaves
    picked
1 tsp cracked black pepper
150ml double cream
Salt and freshly ground
    pepper

Red wine and onion gravy
2 tbsp olive oil
2 onions, finely sliced
2 sprigs of thyme, leaves
    picked
2 tbsp plain flour
300ml red wine
500ml beef stock
2 tbsp caramelised
    onion chutney
1 tbsp Worcestershire sauce
2 tbsp finely chopped
    flat-leaf parsley

1   Preheat the oven to 200°C/180°C Fan/Gas 6. Line a baking
    tray with baking paper.

2   Heat the oil in a large non-stick frying pan over a medium-
    high heat, then add the sausages and brown evenly on all
    sides, turning as necessary. Transfer to the lined baking tray
    and cook on a high shelf in the oven for 15 minutes, turning
    halfway through.

3   Meanwhile, for the mash, put the swede and potatoes into
    a pan half-filled with cold salted water and bring to the
    boil. Lower the heat and simmer for about 20 minutes until
    both veg are tender. Drain in a colander then pass through
    a potato ricer back into the pan (or use a potato masher to
    mash the veg in the pan).

4   Heat the butter in a small saucepan over a medium-high
    heat. When it is melted and foaming, add the garlic, thyme
    and pepper, stir and cook for 2 minutes. Add the cream and
    bring to a gentle simmer. Now pour onto the mashed swede
    and potatoes and stir well. Season with salt to taste.

5   To make the gravy, heat the olive oil in a non-stick sauté pan
    over a medium-high heat. Add the onions and cook, stirring
    often, for 8–10 minutes until golden brown and caramelised.
    Add the thyme and cook for another 2 minutes. Stir in the
    flour and cook, stirring, for 1–2 minutes. Add the wine and let
    bubble to reduce by half then pour in the stock and simmer
    until thickened. Stir in the chutney and Worcestershire sauce.
    Season with salt and pepper to taste.

6   Warm the mash through over a medium heat, then divide
    between warmed serving plates and top with the sausages.
    Spoon on the red wine and onion gravy, scatter over the
    chopped parsley and serve.

Braised short ribs with herby crumb

Beef short ribs require slow cooking because they are full of connective tissue that needs to be broken down for a succulent result. They are carefully prepared in this recipe, to keep them intact. The sharply flavoured pickled shallot garnish and crunchy herby crumb finish the dish beautifully.

Serves 4

4 beef short ribs
  (1.2kg in total)
50g plain flour, plus an extra
  heaped tbsp for the sauce
3 tbsp vegetable oil
2 medium onions, diced
2 medium carrots, diced
3 celery sticks, diced
2 garlic cloves, sliced
2 tbsp tomato purée
300ml red wine
700ml good-quality beef stock
2 tbsp Worcestershire sauce
4 sprigs of thyme
3 sprigs of rosemary
2 bay leaves
Salt and freshly ground
  pepper

Pickled shallots

2 banana shallots, thickly
  sliced
200ml red wine vinegar
80g caster sugar
1 tsp coriander seeds
1 tsp fennel seeds

1 Preheat the oven to 170°C/150°C Fan/Gas 3.

2 Season the beef ribs on both sides with salt and pepper. Put the 50g flour into a shallow bowl and season this too. Tie each beef rib with kitchen string to keep the bone and meat attached.

3 Dip each beef rib into the flour to coat well on all sides. Heat half of the oil in a wide heavy-based ovenproof pan (that has a lid) over a high heat. When it is hot, add the beef ribs and brown well on all sides. Remove from the heat and transfer the ribs to a plate. Wipe out the pan with kitchen paper to remove any burnt bits.

4 Add the remaining oil to the pan and place over a medium-high heat. When hot, add the onions, carrots and celery and cook for 4–5 minutes or until starting to soften. Toss in the garlic and cook for another minute, then stir in the tomato purée and cook for 2 minutes. Add a heaped tbsp flour and cook, stirring, for another minute.

5 Stir in the wine and let it bubble until reduced by half then add the stock and Worcestershire sauce. Tie the thyme and rosemary sprigs together with kitchen string and drop into the pan, along with the bay leaves.

6 Return the browned beef ribs to the pan, bring to a gentle simmer and pop the lid on. Transfer to the middle shelf of the oven and cook for 3 hours or until the beef ribs are tender.

7 Meanwhile, prepare the pickled shallots. Place the shallots in a heatproof bowl. Put the wine vinegar, sugar, coriander seeds and fennel seeds into a small pan. Heat, stirring until the sugar dissolves. Pour this mixture directly over the shallots and leave to stand for at least an hour.

Herby crumb

120g sourdough
30g butter
1 tbsp olive oil
1 tbsp rosemary leaves,
    roughly chopped
2 tbsp chopped flat-leaf
    parsley

8   For the herby crumb, blitz the sourdough in a blender to rough crumbs. Heat the butter and olive oil in a frying pan over a medium-high heat. When the butter is melted and foaming, add the sourdough crumbs and cook until starting to turn golden. Add the rosemary with a good pinch of salt and cook until the crumbs turn a deep golden brown. Remove from the heat and stir through the chopped parsley.

9   When the short ribs are cooked, remove them from the pan and set aside on a plate. Pick out and discard the bunch of herbs and bay leaves. Using a hand-held stick blender, blitz the sauce until smooth. Place the ribs back in the sauce.

10 Serve the ribs with the sauce, on a pile of mashed potato flavoured with mustard. Sprinkle with the herby crumb and finish with a scattering of pickled shallot.

Pictured overleaf

Rib-eye steak Diane with rosemary potatoes

Juicy rib-eye steaks are a great option for a date night in but work equally well cooked on the barbecue. Traditionally, steak Diane specifically calls for Cognac, but any brandy will do in this creamy sauce where the fresh herbs add an important flavour dimension. You will taste the difference if you use locally sourced good-quality beef with great heritage.

Serves 2

2 rib-eye steaks (220g each)
1 tbsp olive oil
2 sprigs of thyme
30g butter
Salt and freshly ground
  pepper

Rosemary potatoes
400g new potatoes, quartered
1 tbsp olive oil
2 sprigs of rosemary, leaves
  picked and finely chopped

Sauce
30g butter
2 banana shallots, finely diced
1 garlic clove, finely chopped
120g baby chestnut
  mushrooms, thickly sliced
40ml brandy
200ml beef stock
2 tbsp Worcestershire sauce
150ml double cream
1 tbsp finely chopped flat-leaf
  parsley or tarragon

1   Take the steaks out of the fridge 30 minutes before you intend to start cooking to bring them to room temperature. Drizzle the steaks with olive oil and season both sides with salt and pepper. Set aside.

2   Preheat the oven to 200°C/180°C Fan/Gas 6. Place the new potatoes on an oven tray, drizzle with olive oil and season with salt and pepper. Toss well and roast in the oven for 20 minutes. Take out the tray, sprinkle the potatoes with the rosemary and toss well. Roast for another 20 minutes or until the potatoes are golden and crispy.

3   Meanwhile, heat a large non-stick frying pan over a high heat. When it is smoking hot, add the steaks and cook for 2–3 minutes on each side, depending on thickness. Remove the pan from the heat and add the thyme, then the butter. Baste the steaks with the butter as it melts. After a couple of minutes, transfer the steaks to a plate, pour over the butter and leave to rest in a warm place.

4   Meanwhile, make the sauce. Place the frying pan back over a medium heat and add the butter. When it is melted and foaming, add the shallots and sauté for 2 minutes. Toss in the garlic and mushrooms and sauté for 3–4 minutes. Now add the brandy, flambé if you like, and let it bubble away.

5   Pour in the stock and simmer until reduced by half. Add the Worcestershire sauce and cream and continue to simmer until the sauce is thickened. Season with salt and pepper to taste and stir through the chopped parsley or tarragon. Add the resting juices from the steak and stir well.

6   Transfer the steaks to warmed plates, spoon on the sauce and serve the crispy rosemary potatoes alongside.

Bavette steak sandwich

Bavette is also known as skirt or flank and it's a tasty cut that needs little time to cook. I season this satisfying steak sandwich with aromatic rosemary, which adds a woody note. The accompaniments are easy: sweet onions, bold blue cheese and a mayo pimped with mustard.

Serves 2

2 bavette steaks (200g each)
1 tbsp light olive oil
1 sprig of rosemary, leaves
    picked and roughly chopped
1 tbsp vegetable oil
20g butter
1 large red onion, thickly
    sliced
2 tsp soft light brown sugar
2 tbsp red wine vinegar
Salt and freshly ground
    pepper

Mustard mayo
3–4 tbsp mayonnaise
1 tsp American mustard
1 tsp English mustard

To assemble
2 ciabatta rolls, halved
    lengthways
2 handfuls of watercress
50g blue cheese

1 Take the steaks out of the fridge about 20 minutes before you intend to start cooking, to bring them to room temperature. Drizzle them with the olive oil and sprinkle with the rosemary and salt and pepper. Set aside.

2 Heat a large non-stick frying pan over a medium-high heat then add the vegetable oil and butter. When the butter is melted and foaming, add the onion and stir well. Cook for 8–10 minutes or until the onion is softened and starting to caramelise. Add the brown sugar and wine vinegar to the pan and stir well until the liquid evaporates. Season with salt and pepper. Remove from the heat.

3 For the mustard mayo, in a small bowl, mix the mayonnaise with both mustards; set aside.

4 When you're ready to serve, heat up a griddle pan over a high heat. When it is smoking hot, add the bavette steaks and cook for 3–4 minutes on each side. Remove from the heat and transfer the steaks to a warm plate. Leave them to rest for a few minutes.

5 Meanwhile, toast the ciabatta rolls, cut side down, on the griddle. When they have a nice char, remove.

6 Spread the bottom halves of the rolls with the mustard mayo and top with the watercress. Cut the bavette into thick slices and lay on top of the watercress. Add a layer of fried onion slices and crumble over the blue cheese. Sandwich together with the ciabatta tops and serve.

Beef smash burgers

In this beefy burger, I cook smashed-down balls of seasoned mince enriched with smoky bacon and sweet, caramelised onions – and the blue cheese topping adds extra punch. I like to give the buns a short steam in the pan because it keeps them lovely and soft.

Serves 4

2 tbsp olive oil
8 rashers of smoked streaky
   bacon
1 large onion, finely diced
500g beef mince
1 tbsp American mustard
1 tbsp tomato ketchup
Salt and freshly ground
   pepper

Burger sauce
4 tbsp mayonnaise
2 tbsp American mustard
2 tbsp tomato ketchup
40g gherkin burger pickle,
   finely chopped

To assemble
4 Blacksticks Blue cheese
   slices
4 seeded or brioche burger
   buns, halved and lightly
   toasted
¼ Iceberg lettuce, shredded
Gherkin pickle slices

To serve
Triple-cooked chips (page 105)
American mustard
Tomato ketchup

1 Preheat the oven to 170°C/150°C Fan/Gas 3. For the burger sauce, mix the ingredients together in a bowl; set aside.

2 Heat 1 tbsp olive oil in a large non-stick frying pan over a medium-high heat. Add the bacon and cook for 3–4 minutes on each side until golden brown and crispy then transfer to an oven tray; keep warm in the oven.

3 Put the pan back over the heat, add the onion and cook for 8–10 minutes until softened and starting to caramelise. Transfer to a large bowl to cool.

4 Once cooled, add the beef mince, mustard and ketchup to the onion. Season generously with salt and pepper and mix well with your hands. Divide into 4 even portions and shape each into a ball.

5 When you're ready to cook, place a large non-stick frying pan (one with a tight-fitting lid) over a high heat. When hot, add the remaining 1 tbsp olive oil to the pan. Now place each ball of meat in the pan, smashing it down with a meat press or strong metal spatula as you add it. Cook for 3–4 minutes or until the burgers have a dark bottom crust.

6 Flip the burgers over and cook on the other side for 1 minute. Top each one with a cheese slice, put the pan lid on and cook for 2 minutes. Lift the lid and place the bun tops on the burgers. Add a splash of water to the pan and re-cover. Heat for 30 seconds – 1 minute.

7 Meanwhile, lay the burger bun bases on serving plates and spread with burger sauce. Add a handful of lettuce and a few gherkin slices. Lay 2 bacon rashers on top. Lift the burgers out of the pan onto the bun bases and press down well. Serve with the rest of the burger sauce in a bowl on the side, along with chips, mustard and ketchup.

Family beef mince pie

This is hearty British comfort food at its best. The pie filling is a classic beefy mixture flavoured with rosemary and thyme – and your family will be suitably dazzled by your efforts with the homemade pastry.

Serves 6–8

Pastry

650g plain flour, plus extra
    to dust
1 tsp sea salt
125g lard, diced, plus extra
    to grease
125g butter, diced
100ml ice-cold water
1 large free-range egg, plus
    an extra beaten egg to glaze

Meat filling

2 tbsp olive oil
30g lard, plus extra to grease
2 large onions, diced
    (275g prepared weight)
2 large carrots, diced
    (285g prepared weight)
3 celery stalks, diced
    (200g prepared weight)
3 garlic cloves, finely chopped
800g beef mince
3 tbsp tomato purée
3 tbsp plain flour
200ml red wine
4 sprigs of thyme
4 sprigs of rosemary
500ml beef stock
2 tsp Bovril
2 tbsp Worcestershire sauce
Salt and freshly ground
    pepper

1. To make the pastry, put the flour into a large bowl with the salt, lard and butter. Using your fingertips, rub the fats into the flour until the mixture resembles breadcrumbs. Add the beaten egg and ice-cold water and mix to combine and form a soft dough. Shape the pastry into a ball, flatten to a large disc and wrap in cling film. Transfer to the fridge and chill for at least an hour.

2. To make the filling, heat half of the olive oil and lard in a large casserole pan over a medium-high heat. Once the lard is melted and foaming, add the onions and carrots and cook for 4–5 minutes. Add the celery and garlic and cook for a further 4 minutes or until all the veg are softened. Scoop them out onto a plate; set aside.

3. Add the remaining olive oil and lard to the pan. When hot, add the beef mince and cook over a high heat until well browned, breaking it up with the back of a wooden spoon. Stir in the tomato purée and cook for 1–2 minutes, then add the flour and cook, stirring, for another 2 minutes. Return the veg to the pan and stir well.

4. Pour in the wine, bring to a simmer and let bubble until it is reduced by half. Tie the thyme and rosemary sprigs together with string and drop into the pot. Pour in the stock and return to a simmer. Lower the heat and cook gently for 30 minutes, stirring occasionally.

5. Add the Bovril and Worcestershire sauce to the beef mix, stir well and season with salt and pepper to taste. Remove from the heat and leave to cool.

6. Preheat the oven to 200°C/180°C Fan/Gas 6. Grease the base of a 26cm round shallow sauté pan with a little lard.

7   Take the pastry from the fridge and divide into 2 pieces: one-third and two-thirds. Dust your work surface with flour and roll out the larger piece of pastry to a 32cm round. Lift into the greased sauté pan and use to line it, pressing it into the corners of the pan and leaving any excess overhanging the edge. Spoon the cooled filling into the pastry case.

8   Roll out the remaining pastry to a 28cm circle. Brush the pastry case edges with beaten egg. Lift the circle of pastry over the filling and press the edges together to seal. Trim off any excess pastry with a sharp knife and crimp the edges.

9   Make a cross in the centre to create a hole large enough to pop in a pie funnel to let the steam escape. Brush the pie well with beaten egg and sprinkle with a little sea salt.

10 Bake in the oven for 40–45 minutes or until the pastry crust turns a deep golden brown. Leave the pie to stand for a few minutes before serving. I love to serve this with some mash and peas on the side.

Pictured overleaf

Lamb loin chops with burnt shallots and peas

This easy recipe is a great reason to tuck into British lamb. Rosemary and lamb are a match made in heaven, as are mint and peas, so I use the whole lot here – along with beautifully caramelised shallots. Be sure to serve this with mash, so all that tasty sauce gets mopped up.

Serves 2–3

6 lamb loin chops
6 shallots, halved
3 garlic cloves, thinly sliced
200ml white wine
400ml lamb stock
120g freshly podded peas
2 sprigs of rosemary, leaves
    picked and finely chopped
1 tbsp red wine vinegar
2 tbsp roughly chopped
    mint leaves
30g cold butter, diced
Salt and freshly ground
    pepper

1   Season the lamb chops on both sides with salt and pepper. Place a large non-stick sauté pan over a medium-high heat. When it is hot, add the lamb chops, fat side down first (to render the fat) for 2–3 minutes. Now lay the chops flat and cook for 3–4 minutes on each side until browned. Remove the chops from the pan and set aside on a tray.

2   Add the shallot halves to the pan, cut side down, and cook for 4–5 minutes until well charred on that side. Turn them over and remove from the pan.

3   Toss the garlic into the pan and cook for 2–3 minutes. Pour in the wine and simmer until reduced by half. Now pour in the stock and cook until the liquor is reduced by half again.

4   Return the lamb chops to the pan and add the peas and rosemary. Simmer for a couple of minutes until the peas are cooked and the chops are warmed through. Remove the pan from the heat. Stir in the wine vinegar and mint and season with salt and pepper to taste. Now stir through the butter to enrich the sauce.

5   Transfer to the chops, shallots, peas and sauce to warmed plates and serve at once, with creamy mashed potato.

Lamb rump with rocket salsa verde

Lamb chops are most people's go-to for the barbecue, but I love the flavour of lamb rump. It's an excellent cut that should be enjoyed heavily browned on the outside and pink in the centre. The accompanying salsa verde is boldly flavoured and includes rocket for some peppery notes.

Serves 4

4 boneless lamb rumps
   (300g each)
3 sprigs of rosemary, leaves
   picked and finely chopped
Salt and freshly ground
   pepper

Rocket salsa verde
2 handfuls of rocket
   leaves (50g)
A handful of basil leaves
A handful of flat-leaf
   parsley leaves
1 small garlic clove,
   finely grated
120ml extra virgin olive oil
2 tsp Dijon mustard
3 tbsp baby capers
1 banana shallot, finely
   chopped
2 tbsp sherry vinegar

1   Preheat the oven to 200°C/180°C Fan/Gas 6.

2   Trim any excess fat from the lamb rumps, leaving a very thin layer of fat on one side. Score the fat with a sharp knife and sprinkle both sides of the rumps with the rosemary and some salt and pepper.

3   Place a large non-stick frying pan over a medium heat and place the lamb rumps in the pan, fat side down. Let the fat render slowly from the lamb and cook for 4–5 minutes until the fat is crispy. Flip the lamb rumps over and cook for another 3–4 minutes.

4   Lift the lamb rumps out of the pan and lay them on an oven tray. Place in the oven for 6–8 minutes, depending on their thickness, to finish cooking.

5   Meanwhile, make the rocket salsa verde. Put the rocket, basil, parsley and garlic into a food processor. Pour in the extra virgin olive oil and blend until smooth. Add the mustard, capers, shallot, sherry vinegar and a good pinch each of salt and pepper. Blend again, very briefly, then transfer the salsa verde to a bowl.

6   When the lamb is ready, remove from the oven and set aside to rest in a warm place for a few minutes. Carve the lamb and serve with the rocket salsa verde, and tenderstem broccoli or some char-grilled courgettes and peppers on the side.

Lamb and chickpea curry

Packed with spice and flavour, this curry is one of my favourites. There is no need to rely on a store-bought curry paste because I use a combination of spices that you likely already have in your store-cupboard. You will taste the difference! Any leftovers will be ace the next day.

Serves 4

1kg lamb neck fillet
3 tbsp vegetable oil
2 large onions, finely diced
4 garlic cloves, finely grated
7.5cm piece of fresh ginger,
   finely grated
1 cinnamon stick
5 cardamom pods
5 cloves
1 tsp cumin seeds
1 tbsp ground coriander
2 tbsp garam masala
1 tsp Kashmiri chilli powder
2 tsp salt
2 tbsp tomato purée
400g tin chickpeas, drained
Coriander leaves, to finish

1   Cut the lamb into 4cm pieces and set aside.

2   Place a large non-stick casserole pan over a medium-high heat and add the oil. When hot, add the onions and cook, stirring often, for 8–10 minutes until softened and turning deep golden brown.

3   Reduce the heat a little and add the garlic and ginger to the pan. Stir over the heat for 2 minutes then add the whole and ground spices, and the salt. Cook, stirring, for a further 2 minutes then add the tomato purée. Stir well and cook for another 2 minutes.

4   Now add the lamb, along with 250ml water, and bring to a simmer. Reduce the heat and pop the lid on. Cook at a gentle simmer for 15 minutes. Remove the lid and give the curry a good stir. Cook, uncovered, for a further 30 minutes, stirring every 10 minutes or so.

5   Tip the chickpeas into the pan, stir into the curry and cook for another 15 minutes or until the lamb is meltingly tender. Taste to check the seasoning and adjust as necessary.

6   Serve the curry scattered with coriander, with some saffron rice or warm naan on the side.

Spiced lamb stuffed tomatoes

This is a fun way to enjoy lamb mince. While it may look like a light meal, it is deceptively satisfying. Large beef tomatoes are used to hold the delicious cooked lamb and rice filling. The addition of dill lifts the flavours further by offering a fresh and fragrant touch.

Serves 6

6 beef tomatoes
2 tbsp olive oil
1 large onion, finely diced
2 garlic cloves, crushed
400g lamb mince
1 tsp ground cumin
½ tsp ground cinnamon
2 tbsp tomato purée
75g easy-cook long-grain
   or basmati rice
300ml lamb or chicken stock
A handful of dill, roughly
   chopped
1 tbsp extra virgin olive oil
Salt and freshly ground
   pepper

1　Slice the top 1cm off each tomato and put these lids to one side. Using a spoon, carefully scoop out the flesh from each tomato, being careful not to break into the skin. Chop the tomato flesh and set aside with any juices. Place the tomato shells on an oven tray.

2　Heat the olive oil in a large sauté pan over a medium-high heat. Add the onion and cook for 5 minutes or until softened and starting to caramelise. Add the garlic and lamb mince and cook, stirring often, for 4–5 minutes or until the lamb is starting to brown.

3　Add the spices and stir over the heat for 1 minute, then add the tomato purée and cook, stirring, for another minute. Tip in the rice and chopped tomatoes with their juice. Pour in 250ml of the stock and bring to a simmer.

4　Pop a lid on the pan and cook for 15 minutes or until the rice is tender and the liquid is fully absorbed. Remove from the heat and leave to cool slightly. Preheat the oven to 200°C/180°C Fan/Gas 6.

5　Stir the chopped dill into the lamb and rice mix and season with salt and pepper to taste. Spoon the filling into the tomatoes and pop the lids on. Drizzle with the extra virgin olive oil and sprinkle with a little salt.

6　Pour the remaining 50ml stock into the oven tray around the tomatoes and bake in the oven for 15 minutes. Remove from the oven and serve warm, with a green salad and some crusty bread alongside.

Lamb shish with garlic and mint yoghurt

This is a nod to a popular takeaway classic we've all enjoyed on the way home from the pub. The kebabs are a great option for your next barbecue, not least because the minty yoghurt brings a coolness to the boldly spiced lamb. With all the accompaniments, it makes for the ultimate messy outdoor feast!

Serves 4

1kg boneless leg of lamb
Salt and freshly ground
   pepper

Marinade
3 garlic cloves, finely grated
1 tsp ground cumin
1 tsp sweet smoked paprika
2 tsp sumac
½ tsp ground cinnamon
1 heaped tbsp Baharat
   spice blend
100g Greek yoghurt

Garlic and mint yoghurt
200g natural yoghurt
1–2 tbsp tahini
Juice of ½ lemon
1 garlic clove, finely grated
A handful of mint leaves,
   finely chopped

To serve
Flatbreads (for homemade
   see pages 20 and 30)
Pickled chillies
Baby cucumbers, cut
   into chunks
Lemon wedges

1   Cut the lamb into 4cm pieces. For the marinade, mix all the ingredients together in a medium bowl. Add the lamb, season with some salt and pepper and toss well. Leave to marinate in a cool place for 1–2 hours.

2   Heat up the barbecue about 25 minutes before you intend to start cooking.

3   For the garlic and mint and yoghurt, mix all the ingredients together in a bowl and season with salt and pepper to taste; set aside.

4   Skewer the marinated lamb onto 4 metal skewers. Cook on the barbecue for around 4–5 minutes on each side until well coloured. Place on a tray to keep warm.

5   Heat the flatbreads quickly on the barbecue until charred in places on both sides.

6   Serve the lamb shish with the warm flatbreads, garlic and mint yoghurt, pickled chillies, cucumbers and lemon wedges.

Roasted chicken thighs with peas

You can't go wrong with succulent roasted chicken thighs and their gloriously crispy skins. This just happens to be my favourite way to enjoy peas and it makes a great family midweek meal. Tarragon and mint feature in the saucy mix and the peas take on these flavours to delicious effect.

Serves 4

8 chicken thighs, bone in
   and skin on
2 tbsp olive oil
2 shallots, halved and sliced
3 garlic cloves, thinly sliced
400ml chicken stock
300g freshly podded peas
3 sprigs of tarragon, leaves
   picked and roughly chopped
2 sprigs of mint, leaves picked
   and roughly chopped
30g cold butter, cut into cubes
Salt and freshly ground
   pepper

1   Preheat the oven to 200°C/180°C Fan/Gas 6.

2   Place a large non-stick sauté pan over a medium heat. Drizzle the chicken thighs with the olive oil and season on both sides with salt and pepper. Place the chicken thighs in the pan, skin side down, and cook for 15–20 minutes or until the skin is a deep golden brown.

3   Transfer the chicken thighs to an oven tray, placing them skin side up. Roast in the oven for 15–20 minutes or until cooked through and the skin is even more crisp.

4   In the meantime, place the sauté pan back over a medium heat. When it is hot, add the shallots and cook, stirring, for 3–4 minutes to soften. Add the garlic and cook for another 2–3 minutes.

5   Pour the stock into the pan, scraping up the bits from the bottom of the pan with a wooden spoon as you do so. Bring the stock to a simmer and let it bubble to reduce by half. Tip the peas into the pan, add the herbs and stir well. Cook for a couple of minutes or until the peas are tender. Add the butter and stir until emulsified into the sauce.

6   Take the tray out of the oven and add the chicken thighs to the sauté pan, tucking them in among the peas. Add the juices from the oven tray too. Stir well and season with salt and pepper to taste.

7   Serve in warmed bowls with rice, mashed potato or even some crusty bread to dip into the delicious sauce.

Roast chicken and potatoes with pan jus dressing

Roast chicken can be enjoyed all year round, but this is no ordinary roast bird.
I season the chicken with oregano and thyme and serve it with potatoes and
Little Gem lettuce. The best part is the delicious dressing made from the roasting
juices, which soaks brilliantly into both the potatoes and lettuce.

Serves 4–6

1 large free-range chicken
   (about 2kg)
3 tbsp extra virgin olive oil
30g butter, softened
3 sprigs of oregano, leaves
   picked and chopped
3 sprigs of thyme, leaves
   picked and chopped
800g medium-small potatoes
1 garlic bulb, cloves separated
   (but not peeled)
Salt and freshly ground
   pepper

Dressing
1 tsp wholegrain mustard
1 tsp Dijon mustard
2 tbsp white wine vinegar

To serve
3 Little Gem lettuce, halved

1   Take the chicken out of the fridge an hour before you intend
    to start cooking, to bring it to room temperature.

2   Preheat the oven to 200°C/180°C Fan/Gas 6.

3   Rub the chicken all over with 2 tbsp extra virgin olive oil and
    the softened butter. Season generously with salt and pepper
    and sprinkle over the chopped herbs. Place the chicken in
    a small roasting tin and roast on a medium-high shelf in the
    oven for 1 hour.

4   Meanwhile, put the potatoes into a separate roasting tin,
    drizzle with the remaining 1 tbsp extra virgin olive oil and
    season with salt and pepper. Roast on the bottom oven shelf
    (below the chicken) for about an hour until crispy on the
    outside but tender inside, when tested with a skewer.

5   Take the chicken out of the oven after an hour and lower
    the setting to 170°C/150°C Fan/Gas 3. Remove any burnt
    bits at the corners of the roasting tin (so they don't go into
    the dressing) then add the garlic cloves to the tray. Give the
    juices a good stir with a wooden spoon, scraping up any bits
    from the base of the tin.

6   Return the roasting tin to the oven and roast the chicken for
    a further 40 minutes or until the skin is golden and crisp and
    the bird is cooked through. To check, insert a skewer into the
    thickest part (between the thigh and body) and check that
    the juices run clear, not pink.

7   When the potatoes are cooked, take out the tray and make
    a small cut in each one. Return the tray to the oven to keep
    the potatoes warm.

8   When the chicken is cooked, set it aside to rest in a warm
    place for around 10 minutes.

9   To make the dressing, put both mustards and the wine
    vinegar into a small bowl and whisk well. Pour about 150ml
    of the juices from the chicken roasting tin into the bowl and
    whisk until you have a smooth, emulsified dressing.

10 Carve the chicken and arrange on a warmed serving platter
    with the Little Gems. Pile the potatoes and soft garlic cloves
    onto another warmed platter. Spoon the dressing over the
    chicken and Little Gems and serve straight away.

Pictured overleaf

Honey and mustard chicken supremes

This recipe calls for chicken supremes – boneless chicken breasts with their wing tip still attached and the skin still intact, giving you succulent breast meat with delightfully crispy skin. The creamy sauce, with its classic combo of honey and mustard, is dead easy to make. A tasty, uncomplicated dish that will likely become a firm family favourite.

Serves 2

2 chicken supremes, skin on
2 tbsp light olive oil
2 banana shallots, finely diced
1 garlic clove, finely chopped
150ml white wine
150ml chicken stock
1 tbsp Dijon mustard
1 tbsp wholegrain mustard
1 sprig of rosemary, leaves
   picked and finely chopped
1 tbsp honey
100ml double cream
Salt and freshly ground
   pepper

1   Preheat the oven to 200°C/180°C Fan/Gas 6.

2   Season the chicken supremes on both sides with salt and pepper. Heat half of the olive oil in a non-stick frying pan over a medium-high heat. Place the chicken supremes in the pan, skin side down, and cook for 8 minutes until the skin is golden brown. Turn the chicken over and cook for 3–4 minutes on the other side.

3   Remove the chicken supremes from the pan and transfer them to a small oven tray. Place in the oven for 8 minutes to finish cooking.

4   In the meantime, make the sauce. Put the frying pan back over a medium-high heat, add the shallots and cook for 3–4 minutes to soften. Add the garlic and cook for another 2 minutes. Increase the heat to high, pour in the wine and let it bubble until reduced by half. Pour in the stock and let bubble until the liquor is reduced by half again.

5   Reduce the heat to medium and add both mustards, the rosemary, honey and cream to the pan. Stir well and simmer gently for 2–3 minutes or until the sauce thickens slightly. Season with salt and pepper to taste.

6   Once the chicken supremes are cooked, remove them from the oven. Serve the chicken with the sauce, and some green beans alongside.

Chicken traybake with garlic and cherry tomatoes

Nothing beats a chicken traybake for a quick and easy midweek meal. I use chicken thighs here, along with plenty of garlic and tomatoes. However, it's the sourdough (which soaks up all those glorious juices) and the delicious combination of herbs that will bring a taste of the Med to your British kitchen.

Serves 4

8 chicken thighs, bone in and skin on (1.5kg in total)
3 tbsp extra virgin olive oil
3 sprigs of oregano, leaves picked and roughly chopped
3 sprigs of rosemary, leaves picked and roughly chopped
200g olive sourdough, cut into 2.5cm cubes
1 garlic bulb, cloves separated (but not peeled)
500g mixed red and yellow cherry tomatoes on-the-vine
100ml chicken stock
2 handfuls of basil leaves
Salt and freshly ground pepper

1. Preheat the oven to 200°C/180°C Fan/Gas 6.

2. Place the chicken thighs in a shallow roasting tray. Drizzle with half of the extra virgin olive oil and season well with salt and pepper. Sprinkle with half of the chopped herbs and turn each chicken thigh over to coat well on both sides.

3. Rearrange the chicken so that all the thighs are skin side up. Place in the oven and bake for 20 minutes.

4. Meanwhile, drizzle the sourdough with the remaining extra virgin olive oil and herbs and toss well to mix. Take the tray from the oven and scatter the sourdough and garlic around the chicken. Return to the oven for 10 minutes.

5. Take out the tray again and tuck the cherry tomatoes around the chicken thighs. Pour over the stock and place back in the oven for another 20 minutes.

6. Remove the tray from the oven and scatter over the basil leaves. Let everyone help themselves to this very easy and super-tasty traybake.

Sticky sesame chicken wings

Marinated in a mixture of honey, soy, garlic and sesame oil, and then baked until deliciously sticky and succulent, these chicken wings are irresistible. The spring onion and roasted sesame seed garnish finishes them off a treat and adds contrasting textures. No cutlery needed!

Serves 4

12 large chicken wings
   (1.5kg in total)
4 garlic cloves, finely grated
4 tbsp tomato ketchup
4 tbsp soy sauce
4 tbsp honey
3 tbsp sesame oil
2 tbsp roasted sesame seeds
3 spring onions, green part
   only, finely sliced, to finish

1   Pat the chicken wings dry with kitchen paper. Put the garlic, tomato ketchup, soy sauce, honey and sesame oil into a medium bowl and whisk well to combine. Add the chicken wings to the bowl, turn them to coat in the mixture and leave to marinate for 1–2 hours.

2   Preheat the oven to 200°C/180°C Fan/Gas 6.

3   Using a slotted spoon, transfer the chicken wings to a large oven tray, placing them in a single layer. Brush half the marinade over them and cook in the oven for 25 minutes.

4   Take out the tray, turn each chicken wing over and brush with the remaining marinade. Place back in the oven and cook for a further 25 minutes.

5   Remove the tray from the oven and sprinkle the chicken wings with the sesame seeds and sliced spring onions. I like to serve these with sticky jasmine rice or a crunchy slaw.

Chicken Kyiv dippers

Chicken tenderloins are the strips of meat you often find attached to the underside of chicken breasts. I use them in these posh crispy strips where I call on the flavours of chicken Kyiv to make a show-stopping dipping sauce featuring garlic, butter, white wine and parsley. What's not to love?

Serves 2

8 chicken tenderloins
200ml buttermilk
1 tsp garlic powder
½ tsp smoked paprika
½ tsp white pepper
120g panko breadcrumbs
Vegetable oil, to fry
Salt and freshly ground
    pepper

Kyiv dipping sauce
125g cold butter, cut into
    cubes
1 banana shallot, finely
    chopped
3 garlic cloves, finely chopped
150ml white wine
3 tbsp finely chopped
    flat-leaf parsley

To serve
Lemon wedges

1. Place the chicken tenderloins in a large bowl and add the buttermilk, garlic powder, smoked paprika, white pepper and a good pinch of salt. Toss well to coat the chicken in the mixture and leave to marinate in a cool place for at least 20 minutes, or up to 2 hours if you have the time.

2. Meanwhile, make the Kyiv dipping sauce. Melt half of the butter in a medium pan over a medium heat. Add the shallot and cook gently for 3–4 minutes to soften, then toss in the garlic and cook for a further 2–3 minutes.

3. Now pour in the wine, increase the heat to high and let it bubble away until reduced by half. Remove the pan from the heat and set aside until needed.

4. Preheat the oven to 180°C/160°C Fan/Gas 4 and set a large wire rack over a baking tray.

5. Tip the breadcrumbs into a shallow bowl. Lift a chicken tenderloin out of the marinade and dip it into the crumbs, making sure it is well coated on all sides, then place on a tray. Repeat with the remaining tenderloins.

6. Heat a 3–5cm depth of oil in a deep sauté pan over a high heat to 170–180°C (check with a thermometer).

7. You will need to cook the tenderloins in batches (to avoid lowering the temperature of the oil). Lower 4 tenderloins into the hot oil and cook for 2–3 minutes on each side or until golden brown all over. Lift them out of the pan with a slotted spoon and place on the wire rack. Pop the tray into the oven to keep warm. Repeat to cook the remaining chicken.

8   Keep the chicken warm in the oven while you finish the
    sauce. Place the saucepan back over a medium heat. When
    the sauce is warm, add a few cubes of butter and whisk to
    emulsify. Whisk in the remaining butter and season with salt
    and pepper to taste. Take the pan off the heat and stir in the
    chopped parsley.

9   Spoon the Kyiv dipping sauce into 2 small bowls and place
    on warmed serving plates. Add the chicken to the plates and
    season with a little extra salt. Add a lemon wedge to each
    plate to serve.

    Pictured overleaf

Dairy

Luscious green pastures are a major part of our British landscape and they're the perfect environment for raising beautiful dairy cows. It takes around two years before a cow is old enough to calve and produce milk – that's a long time to look after them.

It's a very caring industry that you don't really see in any other area of farming, and this is reflected in the quality of the dairy we get here.

The dairy industry has been facing some huge challenges in recent times and continues to do so, but it's still big business – more than 15 billion litres of milk are produced each year in Britain, and we're known all over the world for our incredible dairy products.

As a chef, dairy is an amazing ingredient to work with because it's so versatile. No other ingredient compares with milk when it comes to the range of products you can make with it; it's almost unbelievable.

The huge variation is all down to the fat content – from skimmed milk to yoghurts, creams, custards, ice creams, creamy butters and cheeses – the higher the fat content, the richer and more luxurious it is. We use a lot of dairy in our cooking here in Britain, in much the same way Southern European countries might use olive oil. A knob of butter stirred into a red wine sauce, or a splash of cream added to soup, elevates a dish into something special with very little effort.

Flavour-wise, dairy has an incredible range too. From the unique combination of salty and sharp in cheese that you can use as a seasoning – a little blue cheese with figs (see page 185) or in a pasta sauce (see page 188) perhaps – to a fantastic acidity that cuts through richness, in crème fraîche, buttermilk or soured cream. It's also one of the very few ingredients that works equally well in sweet and savoury dishes – think of a creamy baked cheesecake like the one on page 220, or a rich Cheddar quiche (page 200). Both are decadent, delicious and texturally similar but are found at opposite ends of the menu.

Geographically, the South and Southwest are best suited to dairy cows because of all those lush grassy hills. Cows will eat their way through an entire field in a day! That's why Cornwall and Devon are famous for their clotted cream topped scones, and Cheddar – our nation's most famous dairy export – originates from Cheddar Gorge in Somerset.

Parts of Wales and Scotland also make great farmland for cows and you'll see I've used a Caerphilly cheese in the leek rarebit on page 195. Cows are happy anywhere where there is lots of land for them to roam, and the wet and windy conditions needed for grass to grow. You'll find goats clambering over the mountains in Scotland too – try their produce in the Goat's cheese tartlets on page 180.

We have so much great dairy produce in Britain, which means we also have some amazing classic dairy pairings.

Strawberries and cream is probably the most British dish around. I've included some of our other old-school classic recipes in this chapter too: rice pudding (on page 206), possets (on page 210) and cheese scones (on page 198). But there are also some incredibly talented producers doing impressive things with dairy, influenced by techniques from abroad. I've celebrated this in the garlicky Homemade ricotta on toasted sourdough (page 176).

Along with the quiche, my other favourite recipe in this chapter is the twice-cooked soufflés on page 190. Don't be scared by a soufflé – just don't open the oven door too early!

Homemade ricotta on toasted sourdough

Here's a challenge to impress your mates! Homemade ricotta is not at all complicated: it's a matter of creating curds from a combination of seasoned milk and acidic lemon juice. I serve it here spread thickly on toasted sourdough and rely on the roasted tomatoes and garlic to bring all the flavours together.

Serves 2

Roasted garlic
1 large garlic bulb
1 tbsp extra virgin olive oil
Salt and freshly ground
  pepper

Ricotta
1 litre whole milk
200ml single cream
30–40ml lemon juice

To serve
2 strings of cherry tomatoes
  on-the-vine
2 tbsp extra virgin olive oil
2 slices of sourdough

1   Preheat the oven to 200°C/180°C Fan/Gas 6.

2   Trim the tip off the garlic bulb to expose the top of the cloves then stand it on a large square of foil. Trickle with the extra virgin olive oil, season with salt and pepper and scrunch up the foil around it. Roast in the oven for 30–40 minutes or until the garlic cloves are soft when pressed. Remove from the oven and leave to cool slightly.

3   To make the ricotta, pour the milk and cream into a saucepan and add a good pinch of salt. Place over a medium heat and stir well until it comes to a simmer. Remove from the heat and stir in the lemon juice. Leave to stand for 10 minutes to allow the curds to form.

4   Tip the ricotta curds into a muslin-lined colander to drain then spoon it into a small cheese basket and stand on a tray. Place in the fridge to drain for 30 minutes or so, for a soft ricotta. For a firmer ricotta, leave to drain for a few hours.

5   To serve, preheat the oven to 180°C/160°C Fan/Gas 4. Place the cherry tomatoes on an oven tray and drizzle with 1 tbsp extra virgin olive oil. Season with salt and pepper and pop in the oven for 12 minutes or until soft. Squeeze the flesh from a couple of roasted garlic cloves. (Keep the rest covered with olive oil in a jar in the fridge for other uses.)

6   Brush the sourdough with the remaining extra virgin olive oil. Toast under the grill, or in a dry frying pan over a medium-high heat, until browned on both sides. Spread the toast with the roasted garlic and place on serving plates. Spoon a thick layer of ricotta on top and add a string of roasted tomatoes. Spoon over any pan juices to serve.

Grilled goat's cheese salad

Grilled goat's cheese and beets make a great duo in this sophisticated salad. Pecan nuts and toasted baguette slices offer contrasting textures, and the salad leaves give freshness and vibrancy. A colourful salad, packed with enormous flavours, that works equally well as a starter or light meal.

Serves 2

2 portions of log goat's cheese
   with rind (about 100g each)
1 tsp thyme leaves
1 tbsp runny honey
2 tbsp extra virgin olive oil
6 thick slices of baguette
30g pecan nuts
Salt and freshly ground
   pepper

Maple and mustard dressing
2 tbsp white wine vinegar
1 tsp Dijon mustard
1 tsp wholegrain mustard
1 tbsp maple syrup
3 tbsp extra virgin olive oil

Salad
2 cooked beetroot, cut
   into wedges
½ red onion, thinly sliced
2 large handfuls of mixed
   salad leaves (60g)
A large handful of spinach
   leaves (30g)

1   Preheat the oven to 200°C/180°C Fan/Gas 6. Line a small baking tray with baking paper.

2   Place the goat's cheese portions on the lined tray and sprinkle with the thyme leaves and a little salt and pepper. Drizzle with the honey and 1 tbsp extra virgin olive oil.

3   Brush the baguette slices with 1 tbsp extra virgin olive oil and place on another baking tray with the pecans.

4   Place the goat's cheese tray on a high shelf in the oven and place the baguette and pecan tray on a shelf just below. Bake for 10 minutes, turning the baguette slices and pecans halfway through.

5   Turn the oven grill element on and cook for an extra 2 minutes until the goat's cheese slices are golden brown on top. Take out the other tray as soon as the baguette slices and pecans are well coloured.

6   Meanwhile, prepare the salad. For the dressing, put all of the ingredients into a large bowl, whisk until smooth and season with salt and pepper. Pour half of the dressing into a small serving bowl and set aside. Add the beetroot and onion to the dressing in the large bowl and leave to soak up the flavours.

7   When the baguette and goat's cheese are ready, add the salad leaves to the dressed beetroot and toss well. Divide the salad between 2 serving plates and tuck in the toasted baguettes slices. Top with the baked goat's cheese, scatter over the pecans and serve at once, with the bowl of dressing on the side.

Goat's cheese tartlets

We are spoilt for choice when it comes to great-tasting English goat's cheeses. These lovely tartlets make a charming starter when guests come round. The flavour of the sweet, caramelised shallots cuts through the rich, bold tang of earthy goat's cheese to delicious effect. If you like, you could simplify the recipe by using shop-bought pastry cases.

Makes 8

Shortcrust pastry
300g plain flour, plus
   extra to dust
½ tsp salt
150g cold butter, cut into
   cubes, plus extra (softened)
   to grease
1 large free-range egg

Caramelised shallots
1 tbsp olive oil
20g butter
6 banana shallots, thinly
   sliced
2 tsp thyme leaves
2 tbsp soft brown sugar
1 tbsp red wine vinegar
Salt and freshly ground
   pepper

Béchamel
20g butter
20g plain flour
300ml whole milk
A pinch of freshly grated
   nutmeg
1 tsp wholegrain mustard

To assemble
150g soft goat's cheese log
1 tbsp runny honey

1   To make the pastry, put the flour and salt into a large bowl, add the butter and rub in with your fingertips until the mixture resembles fine breadcrumbs. In a small bowl, beat the egg with 3 tbsp cold water and then pour into the flour mix. Using a table knife, mix to combine and then bring together with your hands to form a dough.

2   Transfer the pastry to a lightly floured surface and knead very briefly until smooth. Shape into a round, flatten to a disc and wrap in cling film. Place in the fridge to rest for an hour.

3   Meanwhile, for the caramelised shallots, heat the olive oil and butter in a medium frying pan over a medium-low heat. Add the shallots and cook gently for about 15 minutes until softened and turning golden. Add the thyme, sugar and some salt and pepper. Cook for a further 10–15 minutes or until the onions are deep brown, soft and jammy. Remove from the heat and stir through the wine vinegar. Leave to cool.

4   Now make the béchamel. Melt the butter in a small saucepan over a medium heat then add the flour and cook, stirring, for 2 minutes. Gradually pour in the milk, whisking continuously until the sauce begins to thicken. Stir in the nutmeg and mustard and season with salt and pepper to taste.

5   Cut 8 thick rounds from the goat's cheese and set aside to use as a topping. Crumble the rest of the cheese into the sauce and stir until melted. Remove from the heat, cover and set aside.

6   Preheat the oven to 190°C/170°C Fan/Gas 5. Take the pastry out of the fridge and leave it to stand for 10 minutes. Lightly grease 8 individual 10cm loose-based fluted tart tins.

7   On a lightly floured surface, roll the dough out until it is about 3mm thick. Cut out eight 12cm circles and gently press each one into a tart tin. Roll a rolling pin over the top of each tin to trim off the excess pastry. Prick the base of each tart case and place in the freezer for 5 minutes to firm up.

8   Place the tart tins on a large baking tray. Line each pastry case with a 12cm round of baking paper then a layer of baking beans. Bake for 15 minutes, then lift out the paper and beans and return the tart cases to the oven for 12–15 minutes until the bases are light golden brown. Remove from the oven and turn the grill element on.

9   Divide the caramelised shallots between the tart cases and level with the back of a spoon. Spoon on a thick layer of béchamel then top each with a slice of goat's cheese. Place back in the oven on a medium-high shelf for 10 minutes. Take the tartlets out and run a cook's blowtorch over the surface of each one for some extra colour.

10   Serve the tartlets warm, topped with a trickle of honey. Serve a bitter leaf salad dressed with a tangy dressing alongside.

Pictured overleaf

Blue cheese and fig toasts

Strong, salty blue cheese and sweet figs are a lovely combination, which I use in these little tapas-style cheese melts. They are effortless to throw together and make a welcome addition to any party spread. Opt for a locally produced cheese if you can – there are plenty of lovely British blue cheeses to choose from.

Makes 12

1 large sourdough baguette
3 tbsp extra virgin olive oil
150g fig chutney
200g blue cheese
6 slices of Parma ham,
  cut in half
A handful of rocket leaves
Salt and freshly ground
  pepper

1   Preheat the grill. Cut the sourdough baguette into 12 thick slices on the diagonal. Lay the slices on an oven tray and brush each with a little extra virgin olive oil. Place the tray under the grill for 2–3 minutes or until golden. Turn and repeat to toast the other side.

2   Spread the sourdough toasts with fig chutney and top each with a slice of the blue cheese; keep the rest for later. Sprinkle with a little salt and pepper. Place the tray back under the grill to melt the cheese and then remove.

3   Place a half slice of Parma ham and a few rocket leaves on each toastie. Transfer to a serving platter and crumble a little blue cheese on top of each one – the perfect bite, enjoy!

Blue cheese dip with potato wedges

This is another crowd-pleasing snack to munch on. The star of the show is the blue cheese dip, which is served here with spiced potato wedges and crunchy celery sticks. However, I suspect you will be using this creamy dip for just about anything: it's tangy, spicy, and packed with herby flavours.

Serves 4 as a starter

Potato wedges
750g potatoes, cut into
    wedges
2 tbsp olive oil
1 tsp garlic powder
1 tsp onion salt
½ tsp smoked paprika

Blue cheese dip
4 tbsp mayonnaise
2 tbsp soured cream
2 tbsp crème fraîche
3 dashes of Worcestershire
    sauce
2 dashes of hot sauce
2 tsp mild American mustard
1 tbsp white wine vinegar
150g blue cheese, crumbled,
    plus an extra 2 tbsp to finish
1 tbsp finely chopped dill
1 tbsp finely chopped chives
Salt and freshly ground
    pepper

To serve
Celery sticks

1   Put the potato wedges into a medium saucepan, pour on cold water to cover and add a good pinch of salt. Bring to a simmer over a medium-high heat and cook for about 7–10 minutes until the potatoes are just tender, not soft.

2   Meanwhile, make the dip. Put the mayo, soured cream, crème fraîche, Worcestershire sauce, hot sauce, mustard and wine vinegar into a small food processor and blitz briefly. Add the blue cheese and blend until smooth. Transfer to a serving bowl, stir through the chopped herbs and season with salt and pepper to taste.

3   When the potatoes are ready, tip them into a colander to drain. Preheat the oven to 200°C/180°C Fan/Gas 6.

4   Trickle the olive oil onto a small ovenproof tray and place in the oven for 5 minutes to heat up. In a small bowl, mix the garlic powder, onion salt and paprika together with 1 tsp salt. Sprinkle half of this spice mix over the potato wedges.

5   When the oil is hot, add the potato wedges to the tray in a single layer and bake for 20 minutes. Remove from the oven, turn the wedges over and sprinkle with the remaining spice mix. Bake for further 20 minutes or until golden and crisp.

6   Place the bowl of blue cheese dip on a platter with the hot potato wedges and celery sticks. Scatter some crumbled blue cheese over the dip and serve straight away.

Blue cheese alfredo

This is a strong-flavoured pasta dish that uses Stilton – our renowned blue cheese, which is made in the Midlands. You will be pleased to know that the inclusion of wine, mustard, Parmesan and strong, punchy sage doesn't take the attention away from the lovely flavour of our beloved Stilton.

Serves 2

250g penne, or other dried
    pasta shapes
16 sage leaves
30g butter
1 tbsp olive oil
2 banana shallots, finely diced
2 garlic cloves, thinly sliced
100ml white wine
100ml chicken or veg stock
1 tsp Dijon mustard
100ml double cream
20g Parmesan, grated
80g Stilton, crumbled
3 tbsp crème fraîche
30g toasted hazelnuts,
    roughly chopped
Salt and freshly ground
    pepper

1   Bring a large saucepan of water to the boil for your pasta and season liberally with salt.

2   Finely chop 6 sage leaves and set aside. Place a medium sauté pan over a medium-high heat and add the butter and olive oil. When the butter is melted and foaming, add the whole sage leaves and cook until crispy on both sides. Remove with a slotted spoon and transfer to a plate lined with kitchen paper to drain.

3   Add the pasta to the boiling salted water, stir well and cook until *al dente* (cooked but still with a bite).

4   Meanwhile, return the sauté pan to the heat and add the shallots and garlic. Cook gently for 3–4 minutes or until the shallots are softened. Add the chopped sage and wine, increase the heat and let bubble until the wine is reduced by half. Add the stock and let this reduce by half too.

5   Add the mustard, cream, Parmesan and two-thirds of the crumbled Stilton to the pan and stir well.

6   Drain the pasta when it is ready, saving half a ladleful of the cooking water. Add the pasta and saved water to the sauté pan and shake it to coat the pasta in the sauce. Add the crème fraîche and stir until you have a silky sauce. Taste to check the seasoning and toss through half of the hazelnuts.

7   Divide the pasta between 2 warmed bowls and scatter over the remaining crumbled Stilton and hazelnuts. Top with the crispy sage leaves and serve.

Twice-cooked cheese soufflés

You'll find it easier to succeed with this twice-cooked recipe than a classic cheese soufflé and it looks just as impressive. I lean on a combination of Cheddar and Stilton here and enhance the mix with mustard. The soufflé is rich and unctuous, so enjoy it with a fresh, green salad on the side.

Makes 4

60g butter, plus extra
   to grease
60g fresh white breadcrumbs
50g plain flour
600ml whole milk
1 tsp English mustard
Freshly grated nutmeg,
   to taste
150g extra-mature Cheddar,
   finely grated
75g Stilton, crumbled
3 large free-range eggs,
   separated
200ml double cream
2 tsp wholegrain mustard
Salt and freshly ground
   pepper

1 Preheat the oven to 200°C/180°C Fan/Gas 6 and place an oven tray inside to heat up.

2 Butter the insides of 4 deep soufflé dishes (240ml capacity). Sprinkle a handful of the breadcrumbs into one dish and turn to coat the base and sides evenly. Tip the excess crumbs into the next soufflé dish and repeat.

3 To make the soufflé base, melt the butter in a saucepan over a medium heat then add the flour and cook, stirring well, for 1 minute to make a roux. Swap the spoon for a whisk and slowly add the milk to the pan, whisking constantly to keep the sauce smooth. Continue to cook, whisking from time to time, until the sauce thickens.

4 Remove the pan from the heat and add the mustard and some nutmeg. Add 100g of the Cheddar and 50g of the Stilton to the pan and mix well. Stir well until the cheese is fully melted. Season with salt and pepper to taste and leave the sauce to cool slightly.

5 Meanwhile, in a very clean bowl, whisk the egg whites together with a pinch of salt until stiff peaks form.

6 Add the egg yolks to the warm cheese sauce base and whisk well. Now add one-third of the whisked egg whites and whisk in to loosen the mixture. Add half of the remaining whisked egg whites and fold in gently, using a large metal spoon or spatula. Repeat to incorporate the rest of the egg whites.

7 Spoon the mixture into the prepared soufflé dishes, dividing it evenly. Take the hot tray from the oven and stand the soufflé dishes on it. Place back in the oven and cook for 12–15 minutes until the soufflés are set.

8   Meanwhile, in a small bowl, mix the cream with the mustard and season with a little salt and pepper. Spoon evenly into 4 individual gratin dishes.

9   Remove the soufflés from the oven and increase the oven setting to 220°C/200°C Fan/Gas 7, turning the grill element on. Run a palette knife around the inside of each dish to loosen the soufflé then gently tip each soufflé into a gratin dish. Mix the remaining Cheddar and Stilton together and sprinkle this over the top of the soufflés.

10 Place the gratin dishes on a high shelf in the oven and bake for 6–8 minutes or until the cheese is golden and bubbling. Remove from the oven and serve at once, with a crispy green salad on the side.

Pictured overleaf

Leek and Caerphilly rarebit

I love Welsh rarebit, and in this recipe I'm flying the Welsh flag even higher by using Caerphilly cheese. I include leeks, which provide a delicate oniony flavour, and cider, which adds a crisp, sweet note. Mustard and Worcestershire sauce provide the sharp and tangy finish.

Serves 2

1 large leek, trimmed and
   washed
1 tbsp olive oil
30g butter
2 sprigs of thyme, leaves
   picked
2 tbsp plain flour
200ml dry cider
1 tsp wholegrain mustard
½ tsp English mustard
1 tsp Worcestershire sauce
150g Caerphilly, grated
1 large free-range egg yolk
1 tbsp finely chopped flat-leaf
   parsley
2 thick slices of sourdough
Salt and freshly ground
   pepper

1. Thinly slice the leek into 5mm thick rounds. Heat the olive oil and butter in a small saucepan over a medium heat. When the butter is melted, add the leek, along with the thyme leaves, and cook for 5 minutes or until completely softened.

2. Add the flour and cook, stirring, for 2 minutes. Gradually pour in the cider, whisking well after each addition to keep the mixture smooth. Continue to whisk gently for a few minutes or until the mixture thickens.

3. Remove the pan from the heat and add both mustards, the Worcestershire sauce and grated Caerphilly. Stir well until the cheese is fully melted. Taste to check the seasoning and add salt and/or pepper as needed. Stir in the egg yolk and chopped parsley then leave to cool slightly.

4. Preheat the oven to 200°C/180°C Fan/Gas 6 with the grill element on. Meanwhile, toast the sourdough on both sides.

5. Lay the toasted sourdough slices on an oven tray and spoon the cheese and leek mixture on top. Place the tray on a high shelf in the oven for 5–8 minutes until the topping is bubbling and golden brown.

6. Remove from the oven and leave to stand for a couple of minutes before transferring the rarebits to warmed plates and tucking in. I like to serve a green salad tossed with a tangy dressing on the side.

British cheese and ale fondue

A retro dish, fondue continues to be popular because the components work so well together. This one uses a variety of English cheeses, along with ale and other strong seasonings. As it's quite robust, I serve the fondue with simple dippers – baguette chunks, diced ham, gherkins and pickled onions.

Serves 6

300ml ale
150ml double cream
1 garlic clove, grated
1 tsp wholegrain mustard
1 tbsp Branston pickle
1 tsp paprika
200g medium Cheddar, grated
100g red Leicester, grated
50g Stilton, crumbled
30g smoked Cheddar, grated
3 tbsp plain flour
80g cream cheese
¼ nutmeg, finely grated
1–2 tbsp finely chopped
   chives
1 tbsp cider vinegar

To serve
200g piece of cooked ham,
   cut into 2cm cubes
150g gherkins
150g pickled onions
1 baguette, roughly torn
   into 2–3cm chunks

1   Pour the ale into a medium saucepan and bring to a simmer. Add the cream and garlic, stir well to combine and return to a low simmer. Let bubble gently for 4–5 minutes, then stir in the mustard, pickle and paprika.

2   Meanwhile, put the grated and crumbled cheeses into a bowl with the flour and mix well. Gradually add this mixture to the pan, a big spoonful at a time, stirring well after each addition.

3   Add the cream cheese and nutmeg to the mixture and stir well to combine. Leave the pan over a low heat while you prepare the sharing board.

4   Place the ham, gherkins, pickled onions and baguette chunks on a large board or in individual bowls to serve alongside your fondue. Provide forks for people to help themselves.

5   Stir the chopped chives and cider vinegar through the warm fondue. Transfer to a warmed fondue pot if you have one, or a warmed dish. This is a great one for sharing!

Cheddar, bacon and herb scones

Served warm, these scones are great at any time of the day. The buttermilk and flour form the base of the scone mix, while the rich Cheddar takes centre-stage along with bacon. The clever combination of hard and soft herbs results in what I think may become your new favourite savoury treat.

Makes 12–15

200g smoked streaky bacon, derinded and finely diced
2 banana shallots, finely chopped
1 tbsp thyme leaves, roughly chopped
1 tbsp rosemary leaves, finely chopped
500g self-raising flour
150g butter, cut into cubes
225ml buttermilk
1 tbsp finely chopped chives
1 tbsp finely chopped flat-leaf parsley
250g Cheddar, grated
Plain flour, to dust
1 free-range egg yolk, to glaze
Salt and freshly ground pepper
Salted butter, to serve

1   Put the bacon into a non-stick frying pan over a medium-high heat for 4–5 minutes until the fat begins to render. Add the shallots, stir well and cook for 4–5 minutes until the bacon is browned and the shallots are softened. Stir through the thyme and rosemary and season well with salt and pepper. Remove from the heat and leave to cool.

2   Meanwhile, put the flour into a large bowl and rub in the butter until the mixture resembles breadcrumbs. Pour in the buttermilk and stir with the handle of a wooden spoon until the mixture starts to come together.

3   Stir the chopped chives and parsley through the cooled bacon mix, then add to the scone mixture with 200g of the grated Cheddar. Season well with salt and pepper and mix lightly to form a dough; don't overwork it.

4   Line a baking tray with baking paper. Tip the dough onto a lightly floured surface and gently roll out until 4cm thick. Using a 6cm plain cutter, cut out rounds and lay on the lined tray. Leave to rest for 30 minutes.

5   Turn each scone over so the flat side is on top and set aside to rest for another 30 minutes. Preheat the oven to 200°C/180°C Fan/Gas 6.

6   Beat the egg yolk with a dash of water and a pinch of salt. Brush the tops of the scones with the egg yolk mix and sprinkle with the remaining cheese. Bake on the middle shelf of the oven for 30–35 minutes or until risen, golden brown and cooked through. Leave to cool slightly.

7   To serve, break the warm scones open and spread with some softened salted butter. Accompany with some onion chutney or even an extra slice of Cheddar if you fancy.

Cheddar quiche

There are massive flavours in this quiche, which uses an easy-to-make shortcrust pastry case. I've held nothing back with the filling: ham, spring onions, herbs, two cheeses, mustard and nutmeg – all in a rich, creamy egg base, further enriched with extra yolks.

Serves 8

Shortcrust pastry
250g plain flour, plus
   extra to dust
1 tsp salt
125g cold butter, diced
1 large free-range egg

Filling
30g butter
4 spring onions, roughly
   chopped
3 sprigs of thyme, leaves
   picked
150g thick-sliced ham, diced
4 large free-range eggs, plus
   an extra 2 yolks
200m double cream
75g crème fraîche
150g strong Cheddar, grated
50g Gouda, cut into small
   cubes
½ tsp freshly grated nutmeg
2 tsp English mustard
Salt and freshly ground
   pepper

1 To make the pastry, put the flour and salt into a food processor, add the butter and pulse until the mixture resembles breadcrumbs. In a small jug, beat the egg with 1 tbsp cold water and pour into the flour mixture. Pulse again until the dough begins to come together.

2 Have ready a 24cm non-stick fluted flan tin, 3.5cm deep. Lift the dough out onto a lightly floured surface, bring it together with your hands and briefly knead it gently until smooth. Then roll out the dough to a circle, 28–30cm in diameter.

3 Gently lift the pastry into the flan tin and use to line the base and sides, pressing it against the inside of the tin with your fingers. Roll a rolling pin over the top of the tin to cut away the excess pastry. Prick the base with a fork and place in the fridge to firm up for 20 minutes.

4 Meanwhile, preheat the oven to 200°C/180°C Fan/Gas 6.

5 Take the flan tin from the fridge. Line the pastry case with baking paper and add a layer of baking beans. Bake on the middle shelf of the oven for 15–20 minutes. Lift out the paper and beans then return the pastry case to the oven for about 10 minutes until the base is light golden in colour.

6 Meanwhile, for the filling, melt the butter into a large sauté pan. When it is foaming, add the spring onions and cook for 2–3 minutes to soften. Add the thyme and ham, cook for another 2 minutes then take off the heat. Leave to cool.

7 Remove the pastry case from the oven and set aside to cool slightly. Lower the oven setting to 190°C/170°C Fan/Gas 5.

8   Put the eggs, egg yolks, cream and crème fraîche into a large bowl and whisk until well combined. Add the cheeses, nutmeg and some salt and pepper and mix again.

9   Spread the mustard thinly over the base of the pastry case and spoon the spring onion and ham mixture evenly on top. Carefully pour in the creamy egg mixture. Stand the tart tin on an oven tray.

10 Bake on the middle shelf of the oven for 25–30 minutes until the filling is golden and just set in the centre. Leave to stand in the tin for a few minutes, then transfer the quiche to a plate or board. I like to serve a salad of tomatoes, finely sliced red onion and basil on the side to cut the richness.

Pictured overleaf

Milk bread burger buns

These milk buns are not only extra special because you baked them, but their soft interior will leave you wanting to make them more often. The buns have a subtle sweetness, but that doesn't mean they can't be part of your burger night. The sesame seed finish leaves them looking *Oh so pro*!

Makes 6

350ml whole milk
20g golden syrup
30g butter
7g sachet instant dried yeast
    (about 1½ tsp)
250g plain flour, plus extra
    to dust
250g strong white bread flour
2 tsp salt
A little oil, to grease

Glaze
1 large free-range egg yolk
1 tbsp whole milk
2 tbsp sesame seeds
    (optional)
Flaky sea salt (optional)

1   Pour the milk into a small saucepan and place over a low heat for 2–3 minutes until just warm. Remove from the heat, add the golden syrup and butter and stir until the butter is melted. Take the pan off the heat. When the milk is warm but not hot to the touch, stir in the yeast and leave for a few minutes to activate.

2   Put both flours into a large bowl, add the salt and mix well. Pour in the warm yeast milk mixture and mix well with your hands until you have a soft dough.

3   Tip the dough out of the bowl onto a lightly floured surface and knead for 5–10 minutes until very soft and springy to the touch. Wipe out the bowl then oil it lightly.

4   Place the dough back in the bowl and cover with cling film or a damp tea towel. Leave to rise for around 30–40 minutes until it is doubled in size.

5   Line a large oven tray with baking paper. Divide the dough into 6 equal pieces and roll each into a ball. Flatten each ball slightly and place on the lined tray. Leave to prove for 25–30 minutes. Preheat the oven to 200°C/180°C Fan/Gas 6.

6   For the glaze, lightly whisk the egg yolk and milk together in a small bowl. Brush the top of each bun with the glaze. Sprinkle with sesame seeds and flaky sea salt, or leave half or all of the buns plain if you prefer. Bake on the middle shelf of the oven for 25 minutes or until deep golden brown.

7   Remove the buns from the oven and leave them to cool slightly. The soft buns are perfect for burgers or anything else you might want to fill them with!

Custardy rice pudding with roasted apricots or plums

This is a beautiful, comforting pudding and it's so easy to make. I toast the rice first, which gives a rich and nutty flavour, and I top the creamy pud with sweet roasted apricots or plums, depending on what's in season. The scattering of toasted almonds finishes it off with a lovely contrasting crunchy texture. If you can get hold of fresh, unpasteurised milk, it will boost the flavour.

Serves 4

180g pudding rice
1 litre whole milk
1 vanilla pod, split lengthways
    and seeds scraped out
3 large free-range egg yolks
100g golden caster sugar
100ml double cream

Roasted fruit

6 apricots or plums, halved
    and stoned
50g soft light brown sugar
Juice of 1 lemon

To finish

4 tbsp clotted cream or
    double cream
30g toasted flaked almonds

1   Preheat the oven to 200°C/180°C Fan/Gas 6 with the grill element on.

2   Put the pudding rice into a dry small frying pan and toast over a medium-high heat for 8 minutes or until the rice grains are lightly toasted.

3   Tip the toasted rice into a medium non-stick saucepan and add the milk and vanilla pod and seeds. Bring to the boil over a medium-high heat and then reduce the heat to a simmer. Cook, stirring every 5 minutes, until the rice is tender; this should take around 20 minutes.

4   Meanwhile, place the apricot or plum halves, cut side up, in a roasting dish and sprinkle with the brown sugar. Wave a cook's blowtorch over the surface to caramelise lightly then place in the oven for 3–5 minutes to soften the fruit slightly. Sprinkle with the lemon juice.

5   In the meantime, whisk the egg yolks and sugar together in a medium bowl until smoothly combined. Add the cream and whisk again.

6   Once the rice is tender, remove the vanilla pod. Add a couple of spoonfuls of rice to the egg mixture and stir it in quickly. Pour this back into the rice pan and stir until well mixed. Place the saucepan back over a low heat and cook gently, stirring, for 5 minutes.

7   Spoon the rice pudding into 4 warmed serving bowls and stir a spoonful of cream through each portion. Top each with a few roasted apricot halves or plums, sprinkle with toasted almonds and enjoy!

Malted milk ice cream

Making your own ice cream might seem intimidating because there is a fine line between gently cooking the eggs (which stabilises an ice-cream base) and scrambling them. However, it is easier to manage than you think. Both kids and adults will love this ice cream's malty flavours... reminiscent of bedtime.

Makes 1.2 litres

700ml whole milk
100g soft light brown sugar
100g golden caster sugar
1 vanilla pod, split lengthways
    and seeds scraped out
80g malt powder (Horlicks)
400ml double cream
5 large free-range egg yolks
150ml malt extract
10 malted milk biscuits
    (80g in total), lightly crushed
A little chocolate syrup,
    to serve (optional)

1   Put the milk, brown sugar and 50g of the caster sugar into a saucepan. Add the vanilla pod and seeds. Place over a medium-low heat and stir gently for 5–10 minutes or until the sugar is dissolved and the mixture comes up to a simmer. Remove the pan from the heat, add the malt powder and stir to dissolve. Set aside.

2   Sit a 2-litre bowl in a larger bowl partially filled with ice and water (to form an ice bath). Pour the cream into the smaller bowl and set a sieve over the top of it.

3   In another bowl, whisk together the egg yolks and remaining 50g caster sugar. Gradually pour on the warm vanilla milk mixture, whisking as you do so. Pour this custard back into the saucepan and place over a low heat. Stir the mixture constantly with a heat-resistant spatula until the custard thickens enough to coat the spatula. Add the malt extract and stir until it is dissolved.

4   Strain the custard into the cream and stir over the ice until cool, then refrigerate to chill.

5   When the creamy custard is well chilled, pour it into an ice-cream machine and freeze according to the manufacturer's instructions. Once thickened, fold through the crushed malted milk biscuits.

6   Transfer the ice cream to a plastic container, cover and place in the freezer for 3–4 hours until frozen solid.

7   When you're ready to serve, scoop the ice cream into serving bowls or waffle cones. A little chocolate syrup trickled over this also works well.

Pink grapefruit possets

These pretty desserts are perfect for a dinner party, and not just because they can be made ahead of time. The creamy posset is topped with a layer of grapefruit jelly – and hidden between the layers is a juicy grapefruit segment. The slightly bitter flavour of grapefruit makes a lovely change from lemon.

Makes 4

2 pink grapefruit
600ml double cream
150g caster sugar
1 vanilla pod, split lengthways
   and seeds scraped out

Jelly topping
3 sheets of leaf gelatine
Juice of 1 pink grapefruit
80g sugar

1   Finely grate the zest from 1 grapefruit and set aside. Now peel this grapefruit with a sharp knife, removing all the pith. Cut out 4 segments; set aside for later. Squeeze the juice from both grapefruit. Strain and measure 150ml for the possets (save the rest for the jelly topping).

2   For the possets, pour the cream into a saucepan and add the sugar and vanilla pod and seeds. Stir over a medium heat until the sugar is dissolved and then allow to simmer for a minute or so. Take off the heat and stir in the grapefruit zest and 150ml juice. Pass through a sieve into a jug and let cool.

3   Pour the cooled posset mixture evenly into 4 serving glasses and place in the fridge for 2–3 hours until set.

4   Meanwhile, make the jelly topping. Place the gelatine sheets in a shallow dish, cover with cold water and leave to soak for 5 minutes until softened. Measure the pink grapefruit juice and add enough of the reserved posset grapefruit juice to make up to 180ml. Pour into a saucepan, add the sugar and stir over a medium heat until the sugar is dissolved. Remove from the heat.

5   Lift out the softened gelatine, squeeze out excess water, then add to the hot grapefruit juice, stirring as you do so. Stir until the gelatine is fully dissolved. Leave to cool.

6   Remove the possets from the fridge and place a grapefruit segment on each one. Carefully spoon on the jelly mixture and put back in the fridge for 30 minutes until the jelly is set.

7   Serve the grapefruit possets, with some shortbread biscuits on the side, if you fancy.

Raspberry ripple ice cream

This make-ahead dessert will delight guests at the end of a summer barbecue.
A standard vanilla ice cream base is boosted with homemade raspberry purée
and the attractive ripple effect is easy to achieve.

Makes 1 litre

250ml whole milk
A pinch of salt
200g golden caster sugar
1 vanilla pod, split lengthways
    and seeds scraped out
500ml double cream
5 large free-range egg yolks
1 tsp vanilla extract

Raspberry sauce
200g raspberries
150g golden caster sugar

To finish
A little whipped cream
A few raspberries

1   Put the milk, salt, sugar and vanilla pod and seeds into a
    saucepan over a medium-low heat and stir gently until the
    sugar is dissolved and the mixture comes up to a simmer.
    Remove from the heat, cover and leave to infuse for 1 hour.

2   For the ice cream, sit a 2-litre bowl in a larger bowl containing
    ice and water (to form an ice bath). Pour the cream into the
    smaller bowl and set a sieve over the top of it.

3   In another bowl, stir the egg yolks until smooth. Re-warm the
    milk then gradually pour a third of it onto the yolks, whisking
    as you do so. Return the mixture to the pan. Cook over a low
    heat, stirring constantly with a heat-resistant spatula until
    the custard thickens enough to coat the spatula.

4   Strain the custard into the cream. Stir until cool, add the
    vanilla extract, then refrigerate to chill, preferably overnight.

5   Pour the chilled mixture into an ice-cream machine and
    freeze according to the manufacturer's instructions.

6   Meanwhile, to make the sauce, put the raspberries, sugar
    and 1 tbsp water into a small saucepan over a low heat to
    dissolve the sugar and bring to a gentle simmer. Pass through
    a sieve, pressing the berries to extract their juice. Return
    to the pan and simmer for 6–8 minutes until reduced and
    thickened. Transfer to a bowl and refrigerate to cool.

7   Spoon half of the ice cream into a plastic container, add
    half of the raspberry sauce and repeat with the remaining
    ice cream and sauce. Now use a table knife to swirl the ice
    cream and ripple the raspberry sauce through lightly. Cover
    and place in the freezer for 4 hours or until frozen solid.

8   Scoop the ice cream into bowls or waffle cones and top with
    a little cream and fresh raspberries to serve.

Yoghurt and apricot parfait with almond praline

I use both natural and Greek yoghurts to achieve the ideal consistency in this parfait. It will serve a small crowd, but you can easily slice off fewer portions when you turn it out and return the rest of the parfait to the freezer for another time. Remember that single apiary regional honey is superior to blended honey.

Serves 10–12

Almond praline
100g flaked almonds
200g caster sugar

Parfait
8 apricots, stoned and
    roughly chopped
Juice of 1 lemon
100ml blossom honey
300ml natural yoghurt
300ml Greek yoghurt
1 vanilla pod, split lengthways
    and seeds scraped out
3 large free-range egg whites
250g caster sugar

To finish
4 ripe apricots, stoned and
    cut into wedges

1 Preheat the oven to 200°C/180°C Fan/Gas 6. Wet the inside of a 1kg (or 2lb) loaf tin with a little water, then line with 2 layers of cling film, leaving some overhanging the edges.

2 For the praline, scatter the almonds on a small baking tray and place in the oven for 8–10 minutes until lightly toasted. Meanwhile, line a heatproof tray with baking paper.

3 Tip the sugar into a small saucepan and place over a high heat. Swirl the pan as the sugar melts and forms a caramel. When the caramel is a deep golden brown colour, add the toasted almonds and stir quickly to coat. Spoon onto the lined tray, flatten with a rubber spatula and leave to cool completely. Once cooled, break off half of the praline, chop it finely and set aside. Save the rest for the decoration.

4 For the parfait, put the apricots into a small saucepan with the lemon juice and honey. Bring to a gentle simmer over a medium heat and cook for 2 minutes to soften the fruit, then remove from the heat. Leave this apricot compote to cool.

5 Place both yoghurts and the vanilla seeds into a large bowl and whisk together until smooth. Add half of the apricot compote to the bowl and mix well.

6 Put the egg whites into the clean, dry bowl of a stand mixer fitted with the whisk attachment. Tip the sugar into a small saucepan, add 50ml water and place over a medium-high heat to dissolve the sugar, then bring to the boil.

7 When the sugar syrup starts to boil, start whisking the egg whites on high speed. Once the syrup registers 117°C on a sugar thermometer (ie the soft ball stage), pour it onto the egg whites in a thin, steady stream, continuing to whisk.

8   When the sugar syrup is all added, turn the mixer speed to medium and whisk the meringue for a further 5–10 minutes or until the bowl is cooled down.

9   Add 2 large spoonfuls of the meringue to the apricot yoghurt mix and whisk to combine. Remove the bowl from the stand mixer. Add half of the remaining meringue and gently fold through the yoghurt, with a spatula. Repeat to incorporate the rest, folding it through until just combined. Finally, fold through the chopped praline.

10 Spoon half of the parfait mixture into the prepared tin. Dollop half of the remaining apricot compote over the parfait and swirl into the mixture. Spoon the remaining parfait mixture into the tin, dollop on the remaining apricot compote and swirl through.

11 Fold the excess cling film over the parfait and place in the freezer for at least 3 hours until firm, preferably overnight.

12 When you are ready to serve, turn the parfait out onto a board or plate and remove the cling film. Top with the apricot wedges and reserved praline, broken into shards. Using a warm knife, cut the parfait into thick slices and serve straight away.

Pictured overleaf

Bay leaf pannacotta with poached peaches

Bay leaves aren't just for savoury cooking. Here, I use their unique flavour to infuse the sweet, creamy pannacotta mixture. I go on to add lemon zest and trusty vanilla to achieve an exciting flavour combination. Serve this dessert in the summer to enjoy the accompanying poached peaches.

Makes 4

4 sheets of leaf gelatine
400ml double cream
250ml whole milk
80g golden caster sugar
6 bay leaves, finely chopped
4 strips of lemon zest (pared
   with a vegetable peeler)
1 vanilla pod, split lengthways
   and seeds scraped out

Poached peaches
100g golden caster sugar
1 tsp vanilla extract
4 bay leaves
2 ripe peaches, halved
   and stoned

1   Place the gelatine sheets in a shallow dish, cover with cold water and leave to soak for 5 minutes or until softened.

2   Pour the cream and milk into a small saucepan and add the sugar, bay leaves, lemon zest, vanilla pod and seeds. Stir over a low heat to dissolve the sugar and cook very gently for 10 minutes. Just before the mixture reaches a simmer, take the pan off the heat and strain through a sieve to remove the vanilla pod, lemon zest strips and bay leaves.

3   Lift out the softened gelatine, squeeze to remove excess water then add to the hot cream mixture, stirring as you do so. Continue to stir until the gelatine is fully dissolved. Pour through a sieve into a jug and leave to cool slightly.

4   Pour the pannacotta mixture evenly into 4 dariole moulds (190ml capacity) and stand them on a tray. Place in the fridge for at least 2 hours or until set.

5   In the meantime, poach the peaches. Pour 300ml water into a small saucepan and add the sugar and vanilla extract. Place over a medium heat and stir until the sugar dissolves. Add the bay leaves and simmer for 3–4 minutes.

6   Lower the peach halves into the sugar syrup and cook for 2 minutes, then lift them out onto a plate. When cool enough to handle, peel away the skin and cut each peach half into 3 wedges. Place back in the syrup until needed.

7   To serve, briefly dip the dariole moulds into a bowl of warm water to come halfway up their sides. Press the top edges of the pannacottas to loosen them and then turn each one out onto a serving plate. Add 3 peach wedges and a bay leaf to each plate and trickle over a little of the syrup.

Baked lemon and ginger cheesecake

The great thing about cheesecake is all the fun you can have flavouring it. In this baked version, I use ginger nut biscuits in the base and add stem ginger, along with its syrup, to the filling. What results is a sharp, spicy dessert that I can only describe as bright!

Serves 10–12

Base
250g ginger nut biscuits
120g butter, melted

Filling
900g cream cheese
200g caster sugar
4 large free-range eggs,
    plus an extra yolk,
    beaten together
2 tsp vanilla paste
Finely grated zest and juice
    of 1 lemon
200g crème fraîche
150g good-quality lemon curd
3 balls of preserved stem
    ginger in syrup, drained
    and finely chopped
3 tbsp stem ginger syrup
    (from the jar)

1   Preheat the oven to 180°C/160°C Fan/Gas 4. Line the base of a 23cm springform cake tin with baking paper: flip the base of the cake tin over and place a piece of baking paper over it, then tuck this into the open springform ring and close it over the base (so the base is flat side up); trim off excess paper.

2   Crush the ginger biscuits in a food processor to fine crumbs (or bash them in a strong plastic bag with a rolling pin). Tip into a large bowl, add the melted butter and mix well. Tip the crumb mixture onto the lined base of your tin and flatten it down evenly, using the base of a glass. Place in the oven for 10 minutes, while you get on with the filling.

3   In a large bowl, beat the cream cheese with a hand-held electric whisk to soften. Gradually add the sugar and eggs and whisk until smooth. Add the vanilla paste, lemon zest and juice, crème fraîche and 100g of the lemon curd. Whisk to combine then stir through the chopped ginger and syrup.

4   Remove the tin from the oven and leave the base to cool slightly. Once it is cooled, pour on the filling. Spoon on the remaining lemon curd and swirl it through the filling.

5   Stand the tin on a baking tray and bake on the middle shelf of the oven for 45–50 minutes – the cheesecake should still have a slight wobble in the middle.

6   Turn off the oven, open the door and leave the cheesecake inside for 30 minutes or so to cool slowly, then transfer to the fridge for an hour to cool completely.

7   When you're ready to serve, run a palette knife around the inside of the tin to loosen the side of the cheesecake, then carefully release it from the tin. Transfer the cheesecake to a serving plate or cake stand and cut into wedges to serve.

Carrot cake with cream cheese frosting

Pulling carrots from the earth is something truly special and they are good all year round. This carrot cake gets the winning combination of carrots, toasted walnuts and warm spices, with a zesty cream cheese frosting, bang-on. You can use this recipe to make muffins or a classic carrot cake (see below).

Makes 12

150g self-raising flour
1 tsp baking powder
1 tsp ground cinnamon
½ tsp ground mixed spice
A pinch of salt
2 large free-range eggs
150g soft light brown sugar
2 tsp vanilla extract
150ml vegetable oil
150g freshly grated carrots
50g toasted walnuts,
   roughly chopped

Cream cheese frosting

225g cream cheese
75g butter, softened
Finely grated zest of
   1 small orange
340g icing sugar, sifted

To finish (optional)

Ground cinnamon
Chopped walnuts

1 Preheat the oven to 180°C/160°C Fan/Gas 4. Line a 12-cup muffin tray with paper muffin cases.

2 Combine the flour, baking powder, spices and salt in a bowl; set aside. Using a stand mixer with the whisk attachment, or a hand-held electric whisk and bowl, whisk the eggs and sugar together for 3–4 minutes or until thick and pale. Add the vanilla extract and oil and whisk for 1 minute.

3 Tip the flour mix into the bowl and whisk briefly to combine. Now fold in the grated carrots and walnuts, using a spatula. Spoon into the muffin cases, dividing the mixture evenly.

4 Bake in the oven for 20 minutes or until a wooden cocktail stick inserted into the centre of one of the muffins comes out clean. Remove the tray from the oven and leave to cool.

5 To make the frosting, in a large bowl, whisk the cream cheese, butter and orange zest together, using a hand-held electric whisk, until smooth. Add the icing sugar gradually, whisking after each addition until it is all incorporated. Cover and refrigerate for 15 minutes to firm up the frosting a little.

6 Once the muffins are cooled, spoon the frosting into a piping bag fitted with a plain nozzle and pipe on top. Sprinkle with a little ground cinnamon and/or chopped walnuts if you like.

Classic carrot cake

Line the base of two 20cm sandwich cake tins with baking paper and oil lightly. Prepare the cake mixture as above, doubling the quantities. Divide the mixture between the cake tins and spread evenly. Bake for 40–50 minutes until a cocktail stick inserted into the centre comes out clean. Cool on a wire rack. Make the cream cheese frosting as above (no need to double up). Once cooled, sandwich the cakes together with half of the frosting and spread the rest on top of the cake. Finish with a dusting of ground cinnamon and a scattering of chopped walnuts if you like.

Fruit

In Britain we grow some of the absolute best seasonal fruit in the world. Starting with rhubarb in spring, through the first sweet strawberries that mark the beginning of our summer, and ending with plums, apples and pears in the autumn.

Even though our fruiting season lasts for only about half the year, we really pack it – in terms of variety – and every few weeks something else is ripe and ready to pick.

Most fruit can also be used in some interesting ways in savoury dishes – in sauces, with meats and with cheeses – but this chapter is all about desserts.

We've always done puddings really well in Britain – maybe it's something to do with having a colder climate. So there are some classic recipes: Blackberry, pear and apple crumble (page 253), Raspberry Victoria sponge (page 246), and Rhubarb jellies (page 230), many served with homemade vanilla custard or cream. They're the tastes of our childhood, with a bit of a grown-up twist.

We often think of soft fruits growing where there's plenty of warm sun, but the flavours are actually sweeter and more intense where daylight hours are longer and temperatures are lower, because the fruits take longer to ripen. That's why in Scotland you'll find the most incredible raspberries, blueberries and strawberries. I've showcased raspberries in a traditional Scottish cranachan (on page 244), laced with whisky and sweetened with honey.

But there's probably nothing that says British summer more than strawberries and cream – maybe with the tennis on the telly – so I've included a couple of recipes that celebrate this dream team: strawberries roasted in Pimm's with vanilla cream and lemon shortbread (on page 238) and a homemade strawberry jelly, custard and cream trifle (on page 240).

Trifle is the perfect combination of everything you want in a pudding: sweetness, richness and acidity from the jelly, flavourful fruit and a rich custard and cream topping. Dairy's luxurious, velvety texture balances the natural acidity and sweetness of fruit really well, so you'll see it a lot in the recipes in this chapter.

Travelling round Britain, the perfect growing conditions for apples and pears are found in Kent and the Midlands. Known globally for their incredible quality, these fruits are crisp and packed with flavour.

Apples are also one of the most versatile fruits and are great for adding moisture and texture to all kinds of cooking.

I've used them in a caramelised apple upside-down cake on page 258 and stewed them with apple brandy on page 257.

Each region can be proud of growing its own fruit, but probably the most localised fruit in Britain is rhubarb. The rhubarb triangle is a tiny nine-square mile area of West Yorkshire that is world-famous for producing forced pink rhubarb. Rhubarb is actually a vegetable, but we treat it like a fruit and it's fantastic poached and served with an almond crumble and vanilla custard enriched with whipped cream on page 228.

However, I think one of the most overlooked fruits that grows very well in Britain are gooseberries. They are outstanding in terms of their flavour, with a high acidity level and fantastic tartness and they're perfect in a classic, creamy Gooseberry fool with ginger biscuits (page 235).

Fools have been made for centuries in Britain and, like all these recipes, have stood the test of time because they demonstrate one of the things we do best when it comes to British fruit: make unbeatably delicious puddings!

Poached rhubarb with almond crumble

Rhubarb is a fabulous British fruit that gets sweeter as you cook it. Here it is served simply with custard and an oaty crumble. If you have any leftover crumble, store it in an airtight container for another time. To make a non-boozy dessert, use pomegranate juice in place of grenadine.

Serves 6

400g trimmed rhubarb,
    cut into 10cm lengths
200ml orange juice
4 tbsp golden caster sugar
4 tbsp grenadine
1 vanilla pod, split lengthways
    and seeds scraped out

Crumble
100g plain flour
100g caster sugar
50g rolled oats
80g butter, diced and
    softened
30g flaked almonds

Vanilla custard cream
250ml whole milk
60g caster sugar
1 vanilla pod, split lengthways
    and seeds scraped out
20g cornflour
4 large free-range egg yolks
300ml double cream,
    softly whipped

1   Preheat the oven to 190°C/170°C Fan/Gas 5 and line a baking tray with baking paper.

2   To make the crumble, put the flour, sugar, oats and butter into a bowl and rub together with your fingertips until the mixture resembles breadcrumbs. Mix in the flaked almonds. Spread the almond crumble out on the lined tray and bake for 10–15 minutes. Give it a good stir and bake for a further 10 minutes or until golden brown. Remove and leave to cool.

3   Lower the oven setting to 180°C/160°C Fan/Gas 4. Place the rhubarb in a large baking dish with the orange juice, sugar, grenadine and vanilla seeds; mix well. Cover the dish with foil and bake for 20–25 minutes or until the rhubarb is tender.

4   Meanwhile, make the vanilla custard. Put the milk into a saucepan with half the sugar and the vanilla seeds and pod. Place over a medium heat until almost steaming. Whisk the remaining sugar, cornflour and egg yolks together in a bowl. Slowly whisk in the milk then pour back into the pan. Whisk over a medium heat for a few minutes until bubbling and thick. Take off the heat, let cool slightly then remove the vanilla pod.

5   If the custard isn't completely smooth, blitz it in a blender to remove any lumps. Pour the custard into a bowl, cover the surface with cling film and refrigerate to cool.

6   Remove the rhubarb from the oven and pour the liquid from the dish into a pan. Simmer over a medium heat until reduced by half. Pour this syrup over the cooked rhubarb and pop back into the oven to keep warm.

7   When ready to serve, tip the cooled custard into a bowl, beat to loosen then fold through the whipped cream. Spoon the rhubarb syrup into serving bowls. Top with the crumble, vanilla custard cream and poached rhubarb to serve.

Rhubarb jellies with vanilla custard

Forced rhubarb is an out-of-season tender, pink rhubarb grown in Yorkshire. The technique used preserves the bright colour and ensures a sweet, less tart flavour. Select the brightest pink stalks you can find to use in this easy recipe to ensure the prettiest result.

Makes 6

Rhubarb jellies
250g trimmed forced rhubarb, cut into 2.5cm pieces
200g golden caster sugar
80ml grenadine
Juice of ½ pink grapefruit
6 sheets of leaf gelatine

Vanilla custard
600ml double cream
1 vanilla pod, split lengthways and seeds scraped out
6 large free-range egg yolks
40g caster sugar

Rhubarb compote
100g golden caster sugar
1 tbsp grenadine
150g trimmed forced rhubarb, cut into 1cm slices

1   For the jellies, have ready 6 dariole moulds (150ml capacity). Put the rhubarb into a saucepan with the sugar, grenadine, pink grapefruit juice and 500ml cold water. Bring to the boil, then lower the heat and simmer gently for 10 minutes until the fruit is soft.

2   Meanwhile, place the gelatine sheets in a shallow dish, pour on enough cold water to cover and leave to soak for 5 minutes until softened.

3   Strain the softened rhubarb through a fine-meshed sieve into a measuring jug, pressing the fruit in the sieve with the back of a spoon to extract as much juice as possible. Leave the strained rhubarb juice to cool. (You can keep the pulp to serve on top of yoghurt.)

4   You'll need 750ml rhubarb juice; if there isn't enough, just top up with water. Pour half the rhubarb juice back into the saucepan and warm over a low heat, then remove. Lift out the softened gelatine, squeeze out excess water and then whisk into the hot rhubarb juice until fully dissolved.

5   Stir the cold rhubarb juice into the hot jelly liquid and leave to cool slightly, then pour evenly into the dariole moulds. Once cooled, refrigerate to set for at least 6 hours, or overnight.

6   Meanwhile, make the vanilla custard. Pour the cream into a medium saucepan, add the vanilla pod and seeds and bring to a simmer over a medium-high heat. Meanwhile, whisk the egg yolks and sugar together in a heatproof bowl until fluffy and pale.

7   Gradually pour the hot vanilla cream onto the egg and sugar mix, whisking constantly, then pour this mixture back into the pan. Place over a low heat and whisk constantly until the custard registers 82°C on a cook's thermometer.

8   Immediately remove from the heat and pass the hot custard through a fine sieve into a bowl. Let cool slightly then cover the surface with cling film and place in the fridge to chill.

9   Meanwhile, make the rhubarb compote. Pour 150ml cold water into a saucepan and add the sugar and grenadine. Bring to the boil over a medium heat, stirring to dissolve the sugar then add the rhubarb. Lower the heat and cook gently for 5 minutes or until tender. Transfer the compote to a serving bowl and leave to cool.

10 When ready to serve, dip the jelly moulds into a bowl of warm water to come halfway up their sides to help loosen them. Turn the jellies out into shallow serving bowls and pour some vanilla custard into each bowl. Serve with the rhubarb compote, and the rest of the custard in a jug on the side.

Pictured overleaf

Gooseberry fool with ginger biscuits

Gooseberries are one of the most underrated fruits in Britain. Granted, they have a short season, so use the opportunity when you can to whip up this easy fool and enjoy their fabulous flavour. Most of your effort goes into the biscuits, but you can make them ahead and keep them in a sealed container for up to a week.

Serves 6

500g gooseberries,
   topped and tailed
100g caster sugar, plus
   an extra 2 tbsp
1 vanilla pod, split lengthways
   and seeds scraped out
500ml double cream

Ginger biscuits
150g self-raising flour
1 tsp bicarbonate of soda
2 tsp ground ginger
1 tsp ground cinnamon
40g caster sugar
40g soft dark brown sugar
50g unsalted butter
2 tbsp golden syrup
1 tbsp treacle

1 First make the biscuits. Preheat the oven to 190°C/170°C Fan/Gas 5. Line 2 large baking trays with baking paper.

2 Sift the flour, bicarbonate of soda, ginger and cinnamon into a large bowl, add both sugars and stir well. Make a well in the centre. In a small saucepan, melt the butter with the golden syrup and treacle, stirring until smooth. Pour the melted mixture into the dry ingredients and mix to a very soft dough.

3 Divide the dough in half. Roll each piece into a log, cut into 8 even discs and roll into balls. Place the dough balls on the trays, leaving a 5cm space in between to allow for spreading. Flatten each ball slightly with your fingers to a disc. Bake for 12–14 minutes or until golden and cracked on top. Remove and leave to firm up on the trays for 10 minutes.

4 Meanwhile, make the fool. Put 400g of the gooseberries into a saucepan with the 100g sugar and vanilla pod and seeds. Bring to a simmer and cook gently for about 10 minutes until starting to soften and break down.

5 Add the remaining gooseberries to the pan and cook for another 5 minutes. Take off the heat, remove the vanilla pod and leave the gooseberry compote to cool completely. (To speed up cooling, transfer to a tray and place in the fridge.)

6 Pour the cream into a bowl, add the 2 tbsp sugar and beat lightly until softly whipped. Add half of the cooled gooseberry compote to the cream and swirl through lightly.

7 Spoon the creamy gooseberry mix into 4 glasses, alternating with the rest of the gooseberry compote. Pop into the fridge until it's time to serve. When you're ready, stand each glass on a plate and serve the ginger biscuits alongside.

Cherry and coconut cake

Cherries have a short and sweet season, so make the most of them. I include coconut in this boozy cake, which adds even more summery feels. Note that a bundt tin is used here; its shape ensures even baking. If you can find one with swirly designs, your work of art will have an even bigger wow factor!

Serves 10

About 300g fresh cherries, pitted and halved (250g pitted weight)
50ml kirsch (or other cherry liqueur)
175g butter, softened, plus extra to grease
225g plain flour, plus an extra 4 tbsp
100g golden caster sugar
75g soft light brown sugar
1 vanilla pod, split lengthways and seeds scraped out
3 large free-range eggs
1½ tsp baking powder
50g desiccated coconut
Finely grated zest of 1 lemon
3 tbsp whole milk
3 tbsp cherry jam

Icing
150g icing sugar, sifted
2 tbsp cherry jam
Juice of ½ lemon

To finish
50g toasted coconut flakes

1   Place the cherries and liqueur in a small bowl and leave to macerate for an hour. Preheat the oven to 180°C/160°C Fan/Gas 4. Grease a 2.4 litre bundt cake tin and dust with 2 tbsp flour, tapping out the excess. Place in the fridge.

2   Using a hand-held electric whisk, or a stand mixer, beat the butter, both sugars and the vanilla seeds together for 3–4 minutes or until the mixture is pale and creamy. Add the eggs, one at a time, whisking well after each addition and scraping down the sides of the bowl with a rubber spatula.

3   Add the 225g flour, baking powder, desiccated coconut, lemon zest and milk, and whisk to combine. Drain the macerated cherries, adding the liqueur to the cake batter; mix again. Toss the cherries with the remaining 2 tbsp flour to coat, then fold through the cake batter.

4   Spoon half of the cake mixture into the prepared tin and dot the cherry jam over the surface. Spoon the remaining cake mixture on top and smooth evenly with the back of a spoon.

5   Stand the cake tin on an oven tray and place on the middle shelf of the oven. Bake for 45 minutes or until the cake is risen and golden, and a skewer inserted into the centre comes out clean.

6   Place the tin on a wire rack and leave to cool for at least 20 minutes before turning the cake out onto a serving plate. If necessary, use a rubber spatula to release it from the tin.

7   To make the icing, in a bowl, mix the icing sugar with the cherry jam, adding the lemon juice a little at a time until the mixture is a spoonable consistency. Spoon the icing over the cake and sprinkle with the toasted coconut flakes to finish.

Roasted strawberries with lemon shortbread

This fun outdoor summer dessert is a nod to the British grass court tennis season. These strawberries are roasted in Pimm's and the flavour is boosted further with mint and vanilla. The accompanying shortbread is an excellent touch with its buttery, crumbly texture and zesty flavour. Freshly picked strawberries will make it extra special.

Serves 4

500g strawberries, hulled
  and halved
150ml Pimm's
1 vanilla pod, split lengthways
  and seeds scraped out
6 sprigs of mint
80g golden caster sugar

Lemon shortbread

125g butter, softened, plus
  extra to grease
80g golden caster sugar, plus
  an extra 1 tbsp to sprinkle
Finely grated zest of 2 lemons
50g ground almonds
150g plain flour
A pinch of salt

Vanilla cream

600ml double cream
2 tbsp golden caster sugar
1 vanilla pod, split lengthways
  and seeds scraped out

1   Preheat the oven to 200°C/180°C Fan/Gas 6.

2   Place the strawberries on an oven tray, pour on the Pimm's and tuck in the vanilla pod and mint sprigs. Mix the sugar with the vanilla seeds and sprinkle over the fruit. Roast on a high shelf in the oven for about 20 minutes until the strawberries are soft. Remove and leave to cool completely. Discard the mint and vanilla pod.

3   For the lemon shortbread, lower the oven setting to 180°C/ 160°C Fan/Gas 4. Lightly grease the base of a 22cm loose-bottomed tart tin.

4   Using a hand-held electric whisk and bowl, or a stand mixer, whisk the butter, sugar and lemon zest together for around 2–3 minutes until light and creamy. Add the ground almonds, flour and salt and stir with a rubber spatula until the mixture begins to come together. Using your hands, bring it together to form a soft dough and pat into a disc.

5   Place the dough in the tart tin and press it down evenly with your hands to fill the tin. Using a sharp knife, cut the dough into 8 wedges. Prick all over with a fork and sprinkle evenly with sugar. Bake in the oven for 30–35 minutes until golden. Remove from the oven and, while still warm, score the wedges again with a sharp knife. Leave to cool.

6   For the vanilla cream, in a medium bowl, whisk the cream with the sugar and vanilla seeds until softly whipped.

7   To serve, divide the vanilla cream between 4 serving plates, make a hollow in the middle and fill with the strawberries and their syrup. Serve at once, with the shortbread wedges.

Strawberry and elderflower trifle

We can't get more British than a strawberry trifle. This one will happily feed a small crowd, making it ideal for summer gatherings where sweet strawberries deserve to be the centre of attention. Elderflower cordial is added to the jelly layer, bringing its own unique floral notes and sweetness.

Serves 8

Jelly layer
200g golden caster sugar
300g strawberries, hulled
   and halved
2 tbsp grenadine
8 sheets of leaf gelatine
5 tbsp elderflower cordial
200g ice cubes

Crème pâtissière
500ml whole milk
1 vanilla pod, split lengthways
   and seeds scraped out
   (or 1 tbsp vanilla paste)
125g golden caster sugar
6 large free-range egg yolks
40g cornflour
250ml double cream

To assemble
300g strawberries, hulled
   and thickly sliced
280g Madeira cake, crust
   removed and cut into
   2.5cm cubes
3 tbsp sherry
400ml double cream
2 tbsp golden caster sugar
1 tbsp vanilla paste
15g toasted flaked almonds

1 To make the jelly layer, pour 500ml water into a medium saucepan, add the sugar and stir over a medium-high heat until the sugar dissolves. Bring to a simmer, then add the strawberries and grenadine and simmer for 10 minutes.

2 Meanwhile, place the gelatine sheets in a shallow dish, add cold water to cover and leave to soak for 5 minutes until softened.

3 Strain the strawberry mixture through a fine-meshed sieve into a heatproof bowl, pressing the fruit in the sieve with the back of a spoon to extract as much juice as possible. Lift out the softened gelatine, squeeze out excess water and then stir into the hot strawberry liquid until fully dissolved. Add the elderflower cordial and ice cubes and stir well.

4 Once the ice cubes have melted and the mixture is cooled, pour the liquid jelly into a large trifle dish (3 litre capacity) and place in the fridge to set.

5 To make the crème pâtissière, pour the milk into a saucepan and add the vanilla (pod and seeds, or paste) and half of the sugar. Slowly bring to a simmer over a low heat. Meanwhile, whisk the egg yolks, remaining sugar and cornflour together in a bowl to combine.

6 Discard the vanilla pod (if used), then gradually pour the hot milk onto the whisked mixture, whisking as you do so. Pour back into the pan and cook over a medium heat, whisking slowly and constantly, for a few minutes until the crème pâtissière is bubbling and thickened. Remove from the heat and leave to cool slightly.

7   Pour the crème pâtissière into a heatproof bowl and cover the surface closely with cling film. Place in the fridge to cool for 2 hours. Towards the end of this time, whip the cream in a separate bowl until firm peaks form.

8   Lightly whisk the cooled crème pâtissière with a balloon whisk to loosen, then add the cream and gently fold together until smoothly combined.

9   To assemble the trifle, once the jelly is set, arrange a ring of strawberry slices on top, around the edge of the bowl. Add the Madeira cake in a single layer and drizzle with the sherry. Add half of the remaining strawberry slices and then spoon over the crème pâtissière. Scatter the rest of the strawberries over the surface and place in the fridge to set.

10 When you are ready to serve, whip the cream, sugar and vanilla paste together in a bowl until soft peaks form. Spoon the whipped cream decoratively on top of the trifle and finish with the toasted almonds.

Pictured overleaf

Raspberry cranachan

Let's raise a glass to the Scots for bringing us what has been referred to as 'the uncontested king of Scottish desserts'. This grown-ups-only summer pud features layers of sweet raspberries, boozy cream and toasted oats. And, since we use Scottish porridge oats, you may as well opt for Scotch whisky too!

Makes 2

20g butter
3 tbsp Scottish porridge oats
2 tbsp honey

Raspberry coulis
150g raspberries
1 tbsp whisky
2 tbsp honey

Vanilla whisky cream
250ml double cream
1 vanilla pod, split lengthways
   and seeds scraped out
1 tbsp honey
1 tbsp whisky

To finish
2 tsp honey (optional)
4 raspberries

1   Melt the butter in a small frying pan over a medium heat. When it starts to foam, add the oats and toast, shaking the pan frequently, for 2–3 minutes or until they begin to colour. Add the honey and stir to combine. Continue to cook until crisp. Remove from the heat and leave to cool.

2   To make the raspberry coulis, put the raspberries into a small saucepan with the whisky and honey. Bring to a simmer over a medium-high heat. Take off the heat and let cool slightly, then tip into a blender and blitz well. Pass through a sieve into a bowl and leave to cool.

3   Meanwhile, to make the vanilla whisky cream, whisk the cream, vanilla seeds, honey and whisky together in a bowl until softly whipped.

4   To assemble the cranachan, spoon half of the raspberry coulis into 2 dessert glasses, then spoon on half of the cream. Scatter half of the toasted oats over the cream. Repeat these layers and add a trickle of honey if you fancy. Finish with a couple of raspberries.

Raspberry Victoria sponge

This British classic was named after Queen Victoria, who, as history tells us, had the ultimate sweet tooth! The moist sponge cake is easy to make and uses only a handful of ingredients, but it's the raspberry that reigns supreme here with both fresh raspberries and raspberry jam in the fruity filling.

Serves 10–12

225g butter, softened,
   plus extra to grease
225g caster sugar
4 large free-range eggs
1 tsp vanilla paste
225g self-raising flour
1 tsp baking powder
½ tsp salt
1 tbsp whole milk

Filling
300ml double cream
2 tbsp caster sugar
1 vanilla pod, split lengthways
   and seeds scraped out
4 tbsp raspberry jam
200g raspberries

1   Preheat the oven to 180°C/160°C Fan/Gas 4. Grease two 20cm round sponge tins and line the base and sides with baking paper.

2   Using a hand-held electric whisk and bowl, or a stand mixer, beat the butter and sugar together for around 3–4 minutes until the mixture is pale and creamy.

3   Add the eggs, one at a time, whisking well after each addition and scraping down the sides of the bowl with a rubber spatula. If the mixture looks as though it is starting to curdle as you add the last of the eggs, whisk in a spoonful of flour.

4   Add the vanilla paste, flour, baking powder, salt and milk, then whisk again until smoothly combined and creamy.

5   Divide the mixture evenly between the prepared cake tins and bake on the middle shelf of the oven for 25 minutes or until risen and golden.

6   Remove from the oven and sit the tins on a wire rack. Let cool for 5 minutes or so and then turn the cakes out and leave to cool completely on the wire racks.

7   Meanwhile, for the filling, in a bowl, whisk the cream with the sugar and vanilla seeds until lightly whipped.

8   Place one cake layer, top side down, on a serving plate or cake stand. Spread with the raspberry jam and then layer the raspberries on top. Spoon the whipped vanilla cream over the raspberries and cover with the second cake layer. Slice the cake into wedges to serve.

Blueberry and ricotta pancakes

Not only are these fluffy pancakes topped with a sweet, tart blueberry sauce, but there are plenty of juicy blueberries hidden right there in the pancake mix itself. Treat your loved one with this special breakfast, which is a fun way to spend a lazy Sunday morning.

Serves 2

2 large free-range eggs,
   separated
125g ricotta
2 tbsp caster sugar
Finely grated zest of ½ lemon
1 tsp vanilla paste
100ml milk
100g self-raising flour
½ tsp baking powder
¼ tsp ground cinnamon
100g blueberries
30g butter

Blueberry sauce
150g blueberries
2 tbsp maple syrup
Juice of 1 lemon
1 tsp vanilla paste
1 tsp cornflour, mixed to
   a paste with 1 tsp water

To serve (optional)
Softly whipped double cream

1   For the pancake batter, in a large bowl, whisk the egg yolks, ricotta, sugar, lemon zest, vanilla paste and milk together using a hand-held electric whisk until smooth. Add the flour, baking powder and cinnamon; whisk to combine.

2   In a separate, very clean bowl, using clean, dry beaters, whisk the egg whites until firm peaks form. Whisk a third into the pancake batter to loosen it then add half the remaining egg whites and fold through gently, using a rubber spatula. Repeat to incorporate the remaining egg whites. Add the blueberries and gently fold into the batter. Set aside.

3   To make the sauce, put the blueberries into a small saucepan with the maple syrup, lemon juice and vanilla paste. Bring to a simmer, stirring, over a medium-high heat and simmer for 2–3 minutes or until the blueberries are tender. Stir in the cornflour paste and cook, stirring, for 1–2 minutes or until thickened. Remove from the heat and leave to cool slightly.

4   To cook the pancakes, place a large non-stick frying pan over a medium heat. Add half of the butter and swirl the pan until it is melted and foaming. Add 3–4 large spoonfuls of the batter to the pan, spacing them well apart. Cook for 2–3 minutes then flip the pancakes over. Cook on the other side for 2–3 minutes until golden brown and puffed up. Lift the pancakes out onto a warmed serving plate.

5   Melt the remaining butter in the pan and cook the remaining batter in the same way. Transfer to a second plate.

6   Spoon the blueberry sauce over the pancakes. I like to serve some whipped cream alongside.

Summer berry tiramisu

We are making the most of British berries in this layered dessert. I realise there isn't a drop of coffee in sight, but my twist on the Italian classic is to use Limoncello, which adds a boozy zing.

Serves 8–10

Berry syrup
Juice of 1 lemon
80g golden caster sugar
100g mixed summer berries (such as strawberries, raspberries, blueberries and blackberries)
80ml Limoncello (lemon liqueur)

Creamy filling
4 large free-range eggs, separated
100g golden caster sugar
250g mascarpone
1 vanilla pod, split lengthways and seeds scraped out
150ml double cream

To assemble
24–30 savoiardi (sponge finger biscuits)
100g raspberries
100g blueberries
150g strawberries, hulled and thickly sliced
100g blackberries, halved
250ml double cream
1 tbsp sugar
2 tbsp Limoncello

1   For the berry syrup, pour 250ml water into a small saucepan and add the lemon juice, sugar and berries. Place over a medium-high heat to dissolve the sugar and let bubble until reduced by one-third. Pass through a sieve into a shallow dish, pressing the fruit in the sieve with the back of a spoon to extract the juice. Stir in the liqueur and set aside to cool.

2   For the creamy filling, in a large bowl, whisk the egg yolks and sugar together using a hand-held electric whisk, for 3–4 minutes until thick and pale. Add half the mascarpone and whisk until smooth, then whisk in the vanilla seeds and the rest of the mascarpone. In another bowl, whisk the cream until thick and then fold through the smooth mascarpone mix.

3   In a very clean bowl, whisk the egg whites until firm peaks form. Stir a large spoonful of the whisked egg whites into the mascarpone cream to loosen it. Add another large spoonful of egg white and carefully fold through using a rubber spatula. Repeat to incorporate the remaining egg whites.

4   To assemble, one at a time, quickly dip half the savoiardi into the berry syrup and use to line the base of a 2.5 litre serving bowl. Spoon over one third of the mascarpone mixture. Set aside 50g of the berries for the topping. Scatter half of the remaining berries over the mascarpone layer. Repeat the savoiardi, mascarpone and berry layers. Finish with a final layer of creamy mascarpone and smooth with a palette knife. Cover and refrigerate for at least 3 hours, or ideally overnight.

5   Pour any leftover berry syrup into a pan and let bubble until reduced to a glaze. Leave to cool. Just before serving, whisk the cream and sugar together in a bowl to soft peaks. Fold in the liqueur and swirl through the berry glaze, if you have it.

6   Spoon the whipped cream over the mascarpone layer and finish with the reserved berries. Serve straight away.

Blackberry, pear and apple crumble

This is the ultimate crumble. In addition to apples (an obvious inclusion since we are famous for our apples), I threw in pears and blackberries. Few things beat the fruity flavour of this warm pud with the crunchy texture of the oat and hazelnut topping. I was fortunate enough to cook and eat this crumble in the orchard where the aroma added to the overall experience and enhanced all the flavours. Lush!

Serves 6

120g butter, diced
100g golden caster sugar
250ml apple and pear juice
2 large Bramley apples,
   peeled, cored and diced
1 Granny Smith or Braeburn
   apple, peeled, cored
   and diced
4 ripe pears, peeled, cored
   and diced
½ tsp ground mixed spice
1 tsp ground cinnamon
300–400g blackberries

Crumble topping
250g plain flour
180g cold butter, diced
60g golden caster sugar
80g rolled oats
100g hazelnuts, roughly
   chopped

To serve
Vanilla ice cream or vanilla
   custard (see page 257)

1 Preheat the oven to 200°C/180°C Fan/Gas 6. Have ready a 32 x 20cm rectangle baking dish and line an oven tray with baking paper.

2 Put the butter and sugar into a sauté pan and place over a medium-high heat for 2–3 minutes or until the butter is melted and the sugar is dissolved. Add the apple and pear juice, bring to a simmer and cook for another 2–3 minutes.

3 Add the Bramley apples to the pan and cook for 5 minutes or until softened. Add the Granny Smith apple and the pears, stir well and cook for another 5 minutes. Remove from the heat and stir in the spices and the blackberries. Transfer the spiced fruit mixture to the baking dish.

4 To make the crumble topping, put the flour and butter into a bowl and rub together with your fingertips until the mixture resembles coarse crumbs. Stir through the sugar, oats and hazelnuts. Sprinkle half of the crumble over the fruit mixture.

5 Scatter the remaining crumble onto the prepared oven tray. Place both the baking dish and tray in the oven and bake for 30 minutes or until the crumble topping on the fruit turns golden brown. Remove the dish and tray from the oven.

6 Spoon some of the crunchy crumble from the tray over the fruit crumble. Serve with vanilla ice cream or custard, with the rest of the crumble in a bowl on the side so everyone can help themselves.

Plum and apple cobbler

This is an uncomplicated recipe that uses the best of Britain's autumnal fruits. Plums are great, and together with the apples, take on all the glorious flavours of the spice mix. I include a little orange zest in the cobbler topping which adds a citrusy note to this utterly British comfort pud.

Serves 6–8

2 large Braeburn apples
10 ripe plums
125g butter
60g golden caster sugar
60g soft light brown sugar
1 vanilla pod, split lengthways
    and seeds scraped out
½ tsp ground cinnamon
½ tsp ground mixed spice
½ tsp ground ginger
2 tsp cornflour

Cobbler topping
200g self-raising wholemeal
    flour
½ tsp baking powder
100g cold butter, diced
85g golden caster sugar
Finely grated zest of ½ orange
80ml single cream
1 large free-range egg

To finish
20g flaked almonds
2 tbsp demerara sugar

To serve
Vanilla ice cream or vanilla
    custard (see page 257)

1   Preheat the oven to 190°C/170°C Fan/Gas 5. Peel, core and roughly chop the apples; halve and stone the plums.

2   Put the butter into a 26cm shallow ovenproof casserole pan and melt over a medium-low heat. Add both sugars to the pan, stir well and heat until the sugar starts to dissolve.

3   Add the apples to the pan and cook for 2 minutes, then add the plums, vanilla pod and seeds and the ground spices. Mix the cornflour with 50ml water to a smooth paste. Pour this into the pan, stir well and then take the pan off the heat. Discard the vanilla pod.

4   To make the cobbler topping, put the flour and baking powder into a large bowl and stir to mix. Add the butter and rub in with your fingertips until the mixture resembles breadcrumbs. Add the sugar and orange zest and stir well.

5   In a small bowl, whisk the cream and egg together until smooth. Add to the dry ingredients and mix until only just combined. Take spoonfuls of the cobbler mixture and dollop on top of the plum mixture, leaving some gaps for the fruit mixture to bubble up around the topping as it bakes.

6   Sprinkle the flaked almonds and demerara sugar over the cobbler topping. Place on the middle shelf of the oven and bake for 35–40 minutes or until the cobbler topping is crisp and golden brown.

7   Remove the cobbler from the oven and serve straight away, with a generous scoop of vanilla ice cream or custard.

Stewed apples with apple brandy and custard

Different apple varieties are celebrated in this comforting pudding, because they each bring their own flavour, sweetness, tartness and texture when cooked. The stewed apple mix is lightly spiced with cinnamon and vanilla. It also includes Calvados, which takes it to another level (but you can replace this with a splash of apple juice if you're serving it up to children).

Serves 4

2 Granny Smith apples
2 Braeburn apples
1 Bramley apple
80g butter
30g golden caster sugar
50g soft light brown sugar
1 cinnamon stick, broken
  in half
1 vanilla pod, split lengthways
  and seeds scraped out
50g raisins
60ml Calvados (apple brandy)

Vanilla custard
600ml double cream
1 vanilla pod, split lengthways
  and seeds scraped out
6 large free-range egg yolks
40g caster sugar

1   Peel, quarter, core and dice all of the apples. Heat the butter and both sugars in a non-stick sauté pan over a medium heat until the butter is melted. Stir well and add the apples, cinnamon, vanilla pod and seeds, raisins and 50ml water. Cook gently for 15–20 minutes or until the apples soften.

2   Stir through the Calvados and cook for another 2 minutes. Remove from the heat and place the lid on the pan to keep the apples warm.

3   Meanwhile, make the vanilla custard. Pour the cream into a saucepan and add the vanilla pod and seeds. Bring to a simmer over a medium-high heat. Meanwhile, whisk the egg yolks and sugar together in a heatproof bowl until pale and fluffy.

4   Gradually pour the hot vanilla cream onto the egg and sugar mix, whisking constantly, then pour the mixture back into the pan. Place over a low heat and whisk constantly until the custard registers 82°C on a cook's thermometer. Pass it through a fine sieve into a warmed jug.

5   Divide the stewed apples and raisins between warmed serving bowls, discarding the cinnamon and vanilla pod. Pour in the vanilla custard to serve.

Apple upside-down cake

The UK has thousands of apple varieties and an increasing number are available to choose from. For this recipe I like to use apples with a high level of acidity, to counteract the sweetness of the caramel. I've gone for Granny Smiths but you can use any other tart apple. Enjoy this cinnamon-spiced cake warm, with a generous scoop of vanilla ice cream.

Serves 8–10

A little softened butter or oil,
  to grease
4 Granny Smith apples

Caramel
150g caster sugar
75g butter, cut into pieces
50ml double cream

Cake mixture
225g butter, softened
225g soft light brown sugar
4 large free-range eggs
2 tsp vanilla paste
225g self-raising flour
1 tsp ground cinnamon
½ tsp ground mixed spice
A pinch of salt

To serve
Vanilla ice cream or softly
  whipped double cream

1   Preheat the oven to 180°C/160°C Fan/Gas 4. Lightly brush a 23cm round loose-bottomed cake tin with soft butter or oil (to help the lining paper stick). Now line the base and sides with baking paper, cutting a 28cm round of paper to line the base to ensure it extends a few cm up the side of the tin. (This will seal the bottom edge and prevent the caramel from spilling out.) Stand the tin on a baking tray.

2   Peel, quarter and core the apples, then cut each apple quarter in half.

3   To prepare the caramel, put the sugar into a small, deep heavy-based saucepan and place over a medium-high heat. As it starts to melt, swirl the pan gently to encourage even melting. When the sugar syrup turns a dark caramel colour, take the pan off the heat and add the butter and cream. The mixture will bubble up at first, so let it calm down and then stir with a wooden spoon. Place the pan back over the heat and stir for 2 minutes until smoothly combined.

4   Carefully pour the caramel onto the base of your lined cake tin. Starting around the edge of the tin, arrange the apple pieces, cut side down, in concentric circles over the caramel, packing them closely together. Set aside while you prepare the cake mixture.

5   Put the butter and sugar into a medium bowl and whisk, using a hand-held electric whisk, until light and creamy. Add the eggs, one by one, whisking well after each addition. (Don't worry if the mixture begins to curdle at this point, once the flour is added it will be ok.)

6   Add the vanilla paste, flour, cinnamon, mixed spice and salt and continue whisking until you have a smooth batter. Spoon the mixture over the apples and smooth over with the back of the spoon to create an even layer.

7   Bake on the middle shelf of the oven for 45–50 minutes. To test, insert a cocktail stick into the middle of the cake – if it comes out clean, the cake is ready. Remove from the oven and leave to stand for 5 minutes to cool a little.

8   Release the cake from the side of the tin. Now invert a large serving plate over the top of the cake and flip both, to turn the cake out onto the plate – do this carefully as there might be some hot caramel sauce under there! Remove the bottom layer of baking paper.

9   Slice the upside-down cake into wedges and serve warm, with a generous scoop of vanilla ice cream or whipped cream on the side.

Pictured overleaf

Poached pear pastries

The classic French dessert of pears poached in red wine inspired these pastries. Every mouthful is an equal hit of soft, spicy pear and crispy pastry. These are best enjoyed warm and will make a lovely treat on an autumn day. Worcestershire is famous for its pears, but any ripe pears will work.

Serves 6

500ml red wine
200g golden caster sugar
1 vanilla pod, split lengthways
   and seeds scraped out
1 cinnamon stick
3 strips of lemon zest (pared
   with a vegetable peeler)
3 ripe pears
325g ready-rolled all-butter
   puff pastry
1 large free-range egg, beaten

Frangipane filling
60g butter, softened
60g golden caster sugar
1 tsp vanilla paste
1 large free-range egg
100g ground almonds
20g plain flour
Finely grated zest of 1 lemon

To glaze
50g flaked almonds
2 tbsp demerara sugar

To serve
Vanilla ice cream or
   cold vanilla custard
   (see page 230–1)

1 Pour the wine into a medium saucepan and add 250ml water, the sugar, vanilla pod and seeds, cinnamon and lemon zest. Bring to a gentle simmer, stirring to dissolve the sugar.

2 Meanwhile, peel the pears, cut in half and scoop out the core, using a melon baller. Add the pear halves to the poaching liquid and cook for 25–35 minutes or until tender. Take off the heat and transfer the pears to a tray to cool slightly, then refrigerate to cool completely.

3 Line a baking tray with baking paper. Lay the puff pastry on a clean surface and cut 6 rectangles, each about 10 x 12cm. Lay them on the lined tray and place in the fridge to rest.

4 To make the frangipane filling, put the butter, sugar and vanilla paste into a bowl and beat with a hand-held electric whisk until pale and creamy. Add the egg and whisk until smooth. Using a spatula or large metal spoon, fold through the ground almonds, flour and lemon zest.

5 Using a sharp knife, score a 1cm border on each pastry rectangle and brush with beaten egg. Prick the inside pastry with a fork. Spoon the frangipane filling onto the pastries, within the border. Slice the pear halves lengthways, keeping them attached at the top. Lay, cut side down, on the filling, fanning the slices out. Chill in the fridge for 20 minutes. Preheat the oven to 200°C/180°C Fan/Gas 6.

6 Brush the pastry border again with egg and sprinkle with the flaked almonds. Sprinkle the demerara sugar over the pastries and bake for a further 20 minutes or until golden brown and cooked through.

7 Serve the pear pastries warm from the oven, with vanilla ice cream or cold custard.

Index

A

ale *see* beer
almonds: almond praline 214
  frangipane 262
  lemon shortbread 238
anchovies: gremolata 124–5
  zesty pork and sage
    meatballs 122
apples: apple upside-down cake
  258–9
  blackberry, pear and apple
    crumble 253
  celeriac soup 69
  fennel and apple slaw 129
  kohlrabi remoulade 60
  pickled cucumber and apple 86
  plum and apple cobbler 254
  stewed apples with apple brandy
    and custard 257
apricots: roasted apricots 206
  yoghurt and apricot parfait
    214–15
asparagus: asparagus, pecorino
    and lemon pasta 24
  asparagus, poached eggs and
    hollandaise 23

B

bacon: bacon and mushrooms eggs
    Benedict 56
  bacon crumb 89
  bacon sauce 86
  beef smash burgers 140
  Brussels sprouts with bacon and
    sage 48
  Cheddar, bacon and herb scones
    198
  cockle chowder 90–1
barbecued pork tomahawk steak
  120

batter, beer 104–5
bavette steak sandwich 138
bay leaf pannacotta 218
béchamel 180
beef: bavette steak sandwich 138
  beef smash burgers 140
  braised short ribs with herby
    crumb 132–3
  family beef mince pie 142–3
  rib-eye steak Diane with
    rosemary potatoes 137
  swede and beef Cornish
    pasties 66
beer: beer battered cod 104–5
  British cheese and ale fondue 196
  Scottish mussels cooked in
    beer 80–1
beetroot: beetroot, mint and
    bulgur wheat salad 59
  grilled goat's cheese salad 178
  pickled radish and sea bass
    crudo 35
biscuits: baked cheesecake 220
  ginger biscuits 235
  lemon shortbread 238
blackberries: blackberry, pear and
    apple crumble 253
  summer berry tiramisu 250
blinis 100
blue cheese: blue cheese
    alfredo 188
  blue cheese and fig toasts 185
  blue cheese dip 186
  blue cheese dressing 32
blueberries: blueberry and ricotta
    pancakes 249
  summer berry tiramisu 250
bread: bavette steak sandwich 138
  chicken traybake with garlic and
    cherry tomatoes 165

flatbreads 20, 30
  gremolata 124–5
  milk bread burger buns 205
  sourdough crumb 47
  tenderstem broccoli and feta
    traybake 50
  see also toast
breadcrumbs: bacon crumb 89
  chicken Kyiv dippers 168–9
  crab cakes 85
  herby crumb 133
British cheese and ale fondue 196
broad bean, ricotta and lemon
  dip 30
broccoli: broccoli and sausage
    pasta 52–3
  tenderstem broccoli and feta
    traybake 50
brown butter and caper sauce 113
Brussels sprouts with bacon and
  sage 48
bulgur wheat: beetroot, mint and
    bulgur wheat salad 59
buns, milk bread burger 205
burgers, beef smash 140
butter: brown butter and caper
    sauce 113
  citrus butter sauce 96
  hollandaise 23, 56
  Kyiv dipping sauce 168–9
  yuzu beurre blanc 114
buttermilk: blinis 100
  Cheddar, bacon and herb
    scones 198
  chicken Kyiv dippers 168–9

C

cabbage: charred hispi cabbage
    with sourdough crumb 47
Cajun crème fraîche sauce 94

cakes: apple upside-down cake 258–9
  carrot cake with cream cheese frosting 223
  cherry and coconut cake 236
  raspberry Victoria sponge 246
Calvados: stewed apples with apple brandy and custard 257
capers: caper mayonnaise 85
  Dover sole with brown butter and capers 113
  rocket salsa verde 149
  tartare sauce 104
caramel: almond praline 214
  apple upside-down cake 258–9
  caramelised pecans 32
carrots: carrot cake with cream cheese frosting 223
  family beef mince pie 142–3
cauliflower: roasted cauliflower cheese 42
cavolo nero: spring greens and feta filo pie 38–9
celeriac soup 69
chard: sea bass baked in a salt crust 110
  spring greens and feta filo pie 38–9
Cheddar, bacon and herb scones 198
Cheddar quiche 200–1
cheese: asparagus, pecorino and lemon pasta 24
  beetroot, mint and bulgur wheat salad 59
  blue cheese alfredo 188
  blue cheese and fig toasts 185
  blue cheese dip 186
  blue cheese dressing 32
  British cheese and ale fondue 196
  Cheddar, bacon and herb scones 198
  Cheddar quiche 200–1

creamy kale pasta with crispy Parmesan 44
  goat's cheese tartlets 180–1
  grilled goat's cheese salad 178
  leek and Caerphilly rarebit 195
  peas with burrata and herb oil 36
  roasted cauliflower cheese 42
  spring greens and feta filo pie 38–9
  tenderstem broccoli and feta traybake 50
  turnip gratin with Lincolnshire Poacher 62
  twice-cooked cheese soufflés 190–1
  whipped feta 20
  see also mascarpone; ricotta
cheesecake, baked lemon and ginger 220
cherry and coconut cake 236
chicken: chicken Kyiv dippers 168–9
  chicken traybake with garlic and cherry tomatoes 165
  honey and mustard chicken supremes 162
  roast chicken and potatoes with pan jus dressing 158–9
  roasted chicken thighs with peas 156
  sticky sesame chicken wings 166
chickpeas: lamb and chickpea curry 150
  red mullet with fennel, chorizo and chickpeas 99
chicory and pear Waldorf salad 32
chillies: steamed razor clams with sherry and fennel 89
chips: layered 'chips' 72
  triple-cooked chips 105
chorizo: red mullet with fennel, chorizo and chickpeas 99
chowder, cockle 90–1

cider: leek and Caerphilly rarebit 195
citrus dressing 36
clams: steamed razor clams with sherry and fennel 89
cobbler, plum and apple 254
cockle chowder 90–1
coconut: cherry and coconut cake 236
cod: beer battered cod 104–5
  crab cakes 85
Cornish pasties, swede and beef 66
crab cakes 85
cranachan, raspberry 244
cream: bay leaf pannacotta 218
  crème pâtissière 240
  gooseberry fool 235
  homemade ricotta 176
  pink grapefruit possets 210
  raspberry Victoria sponge 246
  summer berry tiramisu 250
  vanilla cream 238
  vanilla custard 230–1, 257
  vanilla custard cream 228
  vanilla whisky cream 244
cream cheese: baked lemon and ginger cheesecake 220
  carrot cake with cream cheese frosting 223
crème fraîche: baked lemon and ginger cheesecake 220
  Cajun crème fraîche sauce 94
  mustard crème fraîche 100
  crème pâtissière 240
crumbles: blackberry, pear and apple crumble 253
  poached rhubarb with almond crumble 228
cucumber: pickled cucumber 100
  pickled cucumber and apple 86
curry: lamb and chickpea curry 150
  parsnip purée 65
  roasted cauliflower cheese 42

Scottish mussels cooked in
    beer 80–1
smoked haddock kedgeree 109
custard: custardy rice pudding 206
    vanilla custard 230–1, 257
    vanilla custard cream 228

D

daikon: pickled radish and sea bass
    crudo 35
dairy products 174–5
    see also cheese, cream etc
dips: blue cheese dip 186
    broad bean, ricotta and lemon
        dip 30
Dover sole with brown butter and
    capers 113
dressings: blue cheese dressing 32
    citrus dressing 36
    maple and mustard dressing 178
    pan jus dressing 158–9
    vinaigrette 29

E

eggs: asparagus, poached eggs and
    hollandaise 23
    bacon and mushrooms eggs
        Benedict 56
elderflower cordial: strawberry and
    elderflower trifle 240–1

F

family beef mince pie 142–3
fennel: fennel and apple slaw 129
    fennel salad 102
    red mullet with fennel, chorizo
        and chickpeas 99
    steamed razor clams with sherry
        and fennel 89
fig chutney: blue cheese and fig
    toasts 185
fish 76–7
    see also red mullet, sea bass etc

flatbreads 20, 30
fondue, British cheese and ale 196
fool, gooseberry 235
frangipane 262
frosting, cream cheese 223
fruit 226–7
    see also apples, strawberries etc

G

garlic: broad bean, ricotta and
    lemon dip 30
    chicken traybake with garlic and
        cherry tomatoes 165
    garlic and mint yoghurt 154
    homemade ricotta 176
    roast chicken and potatoes with
        pan jus dressing 158–9
    tenderstem broccoli and feta
        traybake 50
gherkins: tartare sauce 104
ginger: baked lemon and ginger
    cheesecake 220
    ginger biscuits 235
goat's cheese: goat's cheese
    tartlets 180–1
    grilled goat's cheese salad 178
gooseberry fool 235
grapefruit: citrus butter sauce 96
    citrus dressing 36
    pink grapefruit possets 210
    rhubarb jellies with vanilla
        custard 230–1
gratin, turnip 62
gravy, red wine and onion 130
gremolata 124–5

H

halibut with yuzu beurre blanc 114
ham: blue cheese and fig toasts 185
    Cheddar quiche 200–1
    peas with burrata and herb oil 36
hazelnuts: blackberry, pear and
    apple crumble 253

blue cheese alfredo 188
    Brussels sprouts with bacon and
        sage 48
    charred leeks with hazelnuts and
        vinaigrette 29
herb oil 36
herby crumb 133
hollandaise 23, 56
honey: honey and mustard chicken
    supremes 162
    honey roast parsnips 65

I

ice cream: malted milk ice cream
    209
    raspberry ripple ice cream 213
icing 236

J

jelly: pink grapefruit possets 210
    rhubarb jellies with vanilla
        custard 230–1

K

kale: creamy kale pasta with crispy
    Parmesan 44
kedgeree, smoked haddock 109
kirsch: cherry and coconut cake
    236
kohlrabi remoulade 60
Kyiv dipping sauce 168–9

L

lamb: lamb and chickpea curry 150
    lamb loin chops with burnt
        shallots and peas 146
    lamb rump with rocket salsa
        verde 149
    lamb shish with garlic and mint
        yoghurt 154
    spiced lamb stuffed tomatoes
        153
lard: pastry 66, 142

layered 'chips' 72

leeks: celeriac soup 69

    charred leeks with hazelnuts and vinaigrette 29

    cockle chowder 90–1

    leek and Caerphilly rarebit 195

    leek and potato soup 26

    roasted cauliflower cheese 42

    Scottish mussels cooked in beer 80–1

    spring greens and feta filo pie 38–9

lemon: baked lemon and ginger cheesecake 220

    broad bean, ricotta and lemon dip 30

    citrus butter sauce 96

    lemon shortbread 238

limes: citrus dressing 36

Limoncello: summer berry tiramisu 250

M

mackerel with pickled cucumber and blinis 100

malted milk ice cream 209

maple and mustard dressing 178

mascarpone: summer berry tiramisu 250

mayonnaise: blue cheese dip 186

    burger sauce 140

    caper mayonnaise 85

    kohlrabi remoulade 60

    mustard mayo 138

    tartare sauce 104

meat 118–19

    see also pork, lamb etc

meatballs, zesty pork and sage 122

milk: crème pâtissière 240

    custardy rice pudding 206

    homemade ricotta 176

    malted milk ice cream 209

    milk bread burger buns 205

vanilla custard cream 228

mint: garlic and mint yoghurt 154

muffins, carrot cake 223

mushrooms: bacon and mushrooms eggs Benedict 56

    rib-eye steak Diane 137

mussels: Scottish mussels cooked in beer 80–1

mustard: honey and mustard chicken supremes 162

    maple and mustard dressing 178

    mustard crème fraîche 100

    mustard mayo 138

O

oats: blackberry, pear and apple crumble 253

    poached rhubarb with almond crumble 228

    raspberry cranachan 244

oils: herb oil 36

    parsley oil 80

olives: fennel salad 102

    tenderstem broccoli and feta traybake 50

onions: bavette steak sandwich 138

    pickled red onion 102

    red wine and onion gravy 130

    see also shallots

oranges: citrus butter sauce 96

    poached rhubarb with almond crumble 228

oysters two ways 86

P

pan jus dressing 158–9

pancakes, blueberry and ricotta 249

pannacotta, bay leaf 218

paprika sauce 120

parfait, yoghurt and apricot 214–15

Parma ham: blue cheese and fig toasts 185

peas with burrata and herb oil 36

parsley oil 80

parsnips: celeriac soup 69

    honey roast parsnips 65

    parsnip purée 65

pasta: blue cheese alfredo 188

    broccoli and sausage pasta 52–3

    creamy kale pasta with crispy Parmesan 44

pastries, poached pear 262

pastry 66

    shortcrust pastry 142–3, 180–1, 200

peaches, poached 218

pears: blackberry, pear and apple crumble 253

    chicory and pear Waldorf salad 32

    poached pear pastries 262

peas: lamb loin chops with burnt shallots and peas 146

    mushy peas 104–5

    peas with burrata and herb oil 36

    roasted chicken thighs with peas 156

    smoked haddock kedgeree 109

pecans, caramelised 32

pickled cucumber 100

pickled cucumber and apple 86

pickled radish and sea bass crudo 35

pickled red onion 102

pickled shallots 132

pies: family beef mince pie 142–3

    spring greens and feta filo pie 38–9

    swede and beef Cornish pasties 66

Pimm's: roasted strawberries 238

pink grapefruit possets 210

plums: plum and apple cobbler 254

    roasted plums 206

pork: barbecued pork tomahawk steak 120

braised pork jowls with gremolata 124–5

roast pork belly with fennel and apple slaw 129

zesty pork and sage meatballs 122

possets, pink grapefruit 210

potatoes: blue cheese dip with potato wedges 186

cockle chowder 90–1

crispy potato garnish 26

layered 'chips' 72

leek and potato soup 26

ricotta and herb potato bake 70

roast chicken and potatoes with pan jus dressing 158–9

rosemary potatoes 137

scallops with a creamy white wine sauce 78

swede and beef Cornish pasties 66

swede and black pepper mash 130

triple-cooked chips 105

turnip gratin with Lincolnshire Poacher 62

praline, almond 214

Q

quiche, Cheddar 200–1

R

radishes: pickled radish and sea bass crudo 35

rainbow trout with citrus butter sauce 96

rarebit, leek and Caerphilly 195

raspberries: raspberry cranachan 244

raspberry ripple ice cream 213

raspberry Victoria sponge 246

summer berry tiramisu 250

razor clams steamed with sherry and fennel 89

red mullet with fennel, chorizo and chickpeas 99

remoulade, kohlrabi 60

rhubarb: poached rhubarb with almond crumble 228

rhubarb compote 230–1

rhubarb jellies with vanilla custard 230–1

rib-eye steak Diane 137

rice: custardy rice pudding 206

smoked haddock kedgeree 109

spiced lamb stuffed tomatoes 153

ricotta: blueberry and ricotta pancakes 249

broad bean, ricotta and lemon dip 30

homemade ricotta on toasted sourdough 176

ricotta and herb potato bake 70

rocket salsa verde 149

root vegetables 18–19

see also carrots, potatoes etc

rosemary potatoes 137

S

saffron: smoked haddock kedgeree 109

sage: blue cheese alfredo 188

Brussels sprouts with bacon and sage 48

zesty pork and sage meatballs 122

salads: beetroot, mint and bulgur wheat salad 59

chicory and pear Waldorf salad 32

fennel and apple slaw 129

fennel salad 102

grilled goat's cheese salad 178

kohlrabi remoulade 60

salmon with Cajun spices 94

salsa verde, rocket 149

salt crust, sea bass baked in 110

sandwich, bavette steak 138

sardines on toast 102

sauces: bacon sauce 86

béchamel 180

blueberry sauce 249

brown butter and caper sauce 113

burger sauce 140

Cajun crème fraîche sauce 94

citrus butter sauce 96

creamy white wine sauce 78

hollandaise 23, 56

Kyiv dipping sauce 168–9

paprika sauce 120

red wine and onion gravy 130

tartare sauce 104

vanilla custard 230–1, 257

vanilla custard cream 228

sausages: broccoli and sausage pasta 52–3

sausages with swede mash and onion gravy 130

savoiardi (sponge finger biscuits): summer berry tiramisu 250

scallops with a creamy white wine sauce 78

scones: Cheddar, bacon and herb 198

Scottish mussels cooked in beer 80–1

sea bass: pickled radish and sea bass crudo 35

sea bass baked in a salt crust 110

sesame seeds: sticky sesame chicken wings 166

shallots: caramelised shallots 180

lamb loin chops with burnt shallots and peas 146

pickled shallots 132

shellfish 77

sherry: steamed razor clams with sherry and fennel 89

shortbread, lemon 238

shortcrust pastry 142–3, 180–1, 200

shrimps: halibut with yuzu beurre blanc 114

slaw, fennel and apple 129

smoked haddock kedgeree 109

smoked salmon, kohlrabi remoulade with 60

sole: Dover sole with brown butter and capers 113

soufflés, twice-cooked cheese 190–1

soups: celeriac soup 69

cockle chowder 90–1

leek and potato soup 26

sourdough crumb 47

spring greens and feta filo pie 38–9

sticky sesame chicken wings 166

strawberries: roasted strawberries with lemon shortbread 238

strawberry and elderflower trifle 240–1

summer berry tiramisu 250

summer berry tiramisu 250

swede: swede and beef Cornish pasties 66

swede and black pepper mash 130

T

tartare sauce 104

tarts: Cheddar quiche 200–1

goat's cheese tartlets 180–1

tenderstem broccoli and feta traybake 50

tiramisu, summer berry 250

toast: blue cheese and fig toasts 185

homemade ricotta on toasted sourdough 176

leek and Caerphilly rarebit 195

peas with burrata and herb oil 36

sardines on toast 102

tomatoes: chicken traybake with garlic and cherry tomatoes 165

roast tomatoes with whipped feta 20

spiced lamb stuffed tomatoes 153

tenderstem broccoli and feta traybake 50

trifle, strawberry and elderflower 240–1

triple-cooked chips 105

trout: rainbow trout with citrus butter sauce 96

turnip gratin with Lincolnshire Poacher 62

twice-cooked cheese soufflés 190–1

V

vanilla: bay leaf pannacotta 218

cherry and coconut cake 236

crème pâtissière 240

custardy rice pudding 206

gooseberry fool 235

malted milk ice cream 209

pink grapefruit possets 210

poached rhubarb with almond crumble 228

raspberry ripple ice cream 213

roasted strawberries 238

vanilla cream 238

vanilla custard 230–1, 257

vanilla custard cream 228

vanilla whisky cream 244

yoghurt and apricot parfait 214–15

Victoria sponge, raspberry 246

vinaigrette 29

W

Waldorf salad, chicory and pear 32

walnuts: carrot cake 223

watercress: chicory and pear Waldorf salad 32

whisky: raspberry cranachan 244

wine: braised short ribs with herby crumb 132–3

cockle chowder 90–1

family beef mince pie 142–3

honey and mustard chicken supremes 162

Kyiv dipping sauce 168–9

lamb loin chops with burnt shallots and peas 146

poached pear pastries 262

red wine and onion gravy 130

scallops with a creamy white wine sauce 78

yuzu beurre blanc 114

zesty pork and sage meatballs 122

Y

yoghurt: garlic and mint yoghurt 154

whipped feta 20

yoghurt and apricot parfait 214–15

yuzu beurre blanc 114

Z

zesty pork and sage meatballs 122

Thank you!

First off, massive thanks to the whole team at Bloomsbury yet again for creating something magical and special. It never ceases to amaze me how hard everybody works. Once the book is in motion, the hours of dedication from so many people to put things on paper and set it alive is impressive. Thank you to Rowan Yapp, Lena Hall, Janet Illsley, Laura Bayliss, Monya Killian Palmer, Greg Heinimann, Peter Moffat, Ingrid and Tonje at Darling Clementine, Ellen Williams, Helen Upton, Laura Brodie, Di Riley, Rachel Wilkie and Rose Brown.

Nicole Herft, a hero and absolute legend, you and your team constantly make me look good – inspiring, creating and building the most beautiful recipes, and in this case, reflecting the best of Britain. Special mention to Simone Shagam, Becky Wilkinson, Ben Boxall, Anna Colwell, Jake Fenton and Lucy Turnbull.

Capturing the still image but making it feel alive, vibrant and exciting, there isn't anyone better than the magician that is Cristian Barnett and his marvellous team, Lisa Page-Smith and Aloha Shaw. Then tying everything together is Lydia McPherson.

The basis of this book was a food tour of Britain, with me travelling around in a food truck. When the truck was moving (rather than broken down), the content was captured, recorded and edited by the awesome crew from South Shore and Bone Soup television. Thank you all for your dedication and hard work: Rich Bowron, Simon Arnold, Jamie Hammick, Melanie Leach, Andrew Mackenzie-Betty, Leanne Clarke, Ellie Kynaston, Ruth Berkley, Jack Coathupe, Tom Kirkman, George Simpson, Josh Allam and Cath Tudor.

Thank you to the wonderful people at Brand Pilot and Marks & Spencer for helping to deliver, create and build this book and TV series: Heidi Johnson Cash, Amber Stubbings, Frankie Hook, Lisa Fairall, Tom Parson, Rich Robinson, Katy Allison, Katie Hooper, Kate Kennedy, Kate Taylor, Lucinda Knoyle-Hughes, Sharry Crammond, Robbie Black, Kathryn Turner, Jo Webber, Jennifer Meakin, Jess Smith, Laura Davidson, Jessica Jolee, Nate Camponi and Tess Hamilton.

And a shout-out to Borra Garson for guiding me on the book journey.

As always, huge thanks to my Marlow crew. First of all: Bef and Acey for never moaning about me not being there... I'm so sorry I'm away so much. And then there are the incredible people who make my life work: Alex Reilly, Emma Harrand, Warren Geraghty and Alan Dooley. And all the amazing people that work in the pubs and restaurants, who consistently drive and push themselves and their standards forward – you are all brilliant.